LIVES
OF
FAMOUS
ROMANS

Books by Olivia Coolidge

GREEK MYTHS

LEGENDS OF THE NORTH

THE TROJAN WAR

EGYPTIAN ADVENTURES

CROMWELL'S HEAD

ROMAN PEOPLE

WINSTON CHURCHILL AND THE STORY OF TWO WORLD WARS

CAESAR'S GALLIC WAR

MEN OF ATHENS

MAKERS OF THE RED REVOLUTION

PEOPLE IN PALESTINE

LIVES OF FAMOUS ROMANS

LIVES
OF
FAMOUS
ROMANS

OLIVIA COOLIDGE

Illustrated by Milton Johnson

HOUGHTON MIFFLIN COMPANY BOSTON

CONTENTS

use author's prim. sources

LIVES
OF
FAMOUS
ROMANS

Introduction

THE *Lives* of Plutarch, from which we generally gain our knowledge of the great Romans of history, are strictly limited by the age in which they were written and the purpose of the author. Writing for Romans, as Plutarch did, he was concerned as much with the traditions of the race as with its achievements. It was the opinion of the ancients that the purpose of studying history was moral. Lives of famous men were shining examples or alternatively awful warnings. Knowledge of the past, in fact, was good for character.

There is considerable truth in this view in the sense that a nation's traditions have a steadying influence on its citizens. From Plutarch's standpoint, he was right to lay emphasis on the legend of Romulus and Remus or the glorious victories of Scipio Africanus over Hannibal. These have less importance for us today because our interest has shifted. We have our own traditions, heroes, and legends.

It is true that our civilization reaches back to the Roman world and that therefore it is wise to study it. To us, however, it is not the process of Roman history which is important, but the result. The rise of the Romans counts less today than their accomplishments. Romulus and Remus mean nothing personal to us, and Scipio Africanus himself is a foreign general. What we look back to are things like Roman roads, the Roman legal system, architecture, language, ethics, theology even, all the complexities of that Greco-Roman Mediterranean culture which flourished and faded under the Roman Empire.

For reasons of this kind, our point of view is not Plutarch's. We are in addition much better positioned than he to see the panorama of the Roman world unfold and pick out the highlights. Plutarch was born under Nero. He flourished under Trajan and Hadrian at the very beginning of the second century. Roman history, though it was already long, was by no means over. His own age, a brilliant one, had seeds of weakness which were noted at the time but hardly estimated at their true historical value. It looked backward, idealizing the past. It made few prophecies about the future.

For all these reasons, Plutarch, entertaining though he quite frequently is, cannot provide us with sufficient knowledge of the Romans. His list of subjects is wrong. It includes too few of the people who concern us and far too many who do not greatly matter. His method, however, is a good one. The history of the Romans is to a large extent a history of people. The heart of the Empire is Rome, a single city where every important person knows everyone else. It is also a city where character counts for much. Not all Roman character is good. Quite the contrary. Romans are frequently shocking. Interest in character, however, is an enduring quality

among them. It is not by accident that portraiture is their
best form of sculpture.

This being the case, it seemed that Roman history might
be presented as Plutarch did it, but with a different object.
He spoke to his day, we to ours. What is vital to us may not
be to him. We differ in knowledge, in critical habits, in style
and organization. He need not fear the challenge. His reputation is assured in any case. His literary merits are considerable ones. No doubt Plutarch will always be enjoyed. Our
mistake is to take him as our exclusive guide through Roman
history.

CICERO

Marcus Tullius Cicero, 106–43 B.C.

ENTHUSIASTIC, brilliant, emotional, Cicero reminds us of an Italian rather than the severer Roman. It is fitting that he should, for he came from the town of Arpinum in the Volscian hills a little distance from Rome. At the time of her earliest conquests, Rome had been generous with her citizenship. It was therefore possible for a boy from Arpinum to look forward to a political career instead of vegetating quietly at home or engaging in trade. It is true that the Roman-born aristocrats who dominated the later Republic had a prejudice against newcomers, particularly if they were not native Romans. It happened, however, that in the year before Cicero's birth a native of Arpinum had risen to the very top. Caius Marius, who became consul in 107 B.C., was a dominating figure at Rome for the first twenty years of Cicero's life. His little township, which made up for its obscurity by an intense local patriotism, followed the fortunes of its famous son with breathless interest. Marius, not even from one of the best families in town, had leaped over all barriers to success. The feat was possible, and the imagination of a younger boy with great abilities was fired.

It is difficult to overestimate the influence of Marius on his home town of Arpinum. Cicero's father, a man of decent abilities and good position, had aspired to no rank in Rome. Yet Cicero, as well as his younger brother, and his cousins were all brought up to think of a Roman career. In preparation, they were carefully educated at home, sent to Greece for further study, and encouraged to acquire a very wide culture. Cicero's talents were early evident, and his father had connections in Rome among distinguished people. It was always obvious that the boy would serve a year in the army as junior officer for experience's sake, and then study Roman law.

Caius Marius had been simply and solely a great soldier. His work was the reform of the Roman army. Earlier conquests had been made by the Italian citizen-soldier. Farmers drafted for a campaigning season had left home after the grain was in the ground and had returned for the late plowing. By 107 B.C., however, campaigns were all abroad and apt to last several years. There was not much fighting in winter, to be sure; but armies could not just go home. Bigger forces were necessary, too, requiring more complex training in maneuver. In short, Rome needed professional armies; and it was the function of Marius to supply them.

Cicero's own gifts were not military ones, yet the new Roman armies affected his career from the very outset. Marius had taught his successors how to raise and train soldiers. The insoluble problem became how to demobilize them. When a general was entrusted by the Senate with a campaign, he was given permission to raise a certain number of legions. Pay was granted for the duration only, after which the army was supposed to be disbanded. Under the new conditions, however, enlisted soldiers were adventurers without a home to go back to. Their general had invariably promised to get a law passed providing some sort of severance pay, usually a farm. Thus the political power of their general was vital to his soldiers, who were ready to support it by force. Major victory abroad too often resulted in dictatorship or civil war at home.

This was the pattern established by Marius, who perished in 86 B.C. during the course of a civil war with Sulla, a rival general who had copied Marius's methods. Sulla took elaborate vengeance on Marius's partisans, publishing lists of those for whose death reward was offered. It was frighteningly easy to get a name placed on those proscription lists if one had influence in the right quarters. Twenty-year-old Cicero, burning to make his debut, might not be in danger as yet. Clearly, however, it would be risky to bring Arpinum back into the news. To the budding genius from Marius's home town, the perils of success had become far greater than its opportunities.

Cicero never lacked courage. Six years later when he was already beginning to be heard in the law courts, a case came up which none of the older advocates dared undertake. Though risky for them, it must have been far more so for the new young man with the suspicious background. Sulla's proscription had by now exhausted itself, but his dictatorship remained absolute and rigid. Nobody dared criticize, even in cases of injustice.

Sextius Roscius, a wealthy citizen of Ameria who had fought in Sulla's army, had come after his victory to Rome. The city was full of organized gangs who were hunting down proscribed victims for the sake of the blood money promised by the government. Crime breeds crime. Sextius Roscius was murdered by some distant kinsmen as he walked home after supper. The murderers bribed Chrysogonus, a favorite servant and ex-slave of Sulla's, to enter Roscius's name on the proscription lists. As a result, his property was confiscated and sold to Chrysogonus for a song, nobody daring to bid against him. Chrysogonus then made the murderers his agents and employed them to dispossess the only son of Roscius. The criminals divided up their profits, but they soon became worried lest times change and the young Roscius call them to account. By now the proscriptions were over, and it was less easy to assassinate a man or cover up murder. They therefore tried to get rid of Roscius by accusing him of the murder of his father. No one, they reckoned, would dare bring out the facts, since to accuse Chrysogonus would be almost as dangerous as attacking Sulla.

To take such a case required both skill and daring. The truth had been hushed up, and if possible the jury would prefer not to be enlightened. Cicero's youth was against him, as was his background. Only by speaking out with the utmost frankness could he win, yet he must do so without offending the all-powerful dictator.

Cicero's genius proved equal to the task. Skillfully he excused Sulla while pressing home the charge against his servant. Roscius was acquitted, and Cicero found himself famous. But while Sulla could hardly avenge his servant in so notorious a case, it was only a question of time until he found a chance of getting even. It would have been folly for Cicero to continue legal practice, and it so happened that he had strained his voice. Friends even told him that he would have to give up public speaking altogether. Instead of doing so, he went to Rhodes for a couple of years to study voice production. Most fortunately for him, Sulla died in 78 of a seizure. Legend has it that a pair of his boots did not fit. Sulla ordered the maker to be flogged to death before his eyes, and he died of rage. At all events, young Cicero was able to return to Rome before the public had forgotten all about him. As a consequence, he was soon elected Quaestor and departed for a year of administration in Sicily. Returning, he became as an automatic next step a member of the Senate. He was thirty-two, and a new age was dawning. Cicero as much as any other man would set his mark on it.

He had done well in Sicily and thought that the eyes of his world were on him. It was a shock to discover that fashionable Rome knew nothing of what he had accomplished. He tells the story of his dismay to get a frank laugh, yet there is more behind it than a young man's naïve conceit. Fame in the law courts had never been more than a means to an end. The boy from Arpinum had now won his place in the governing body which ruled, through Rome, the world. It was not often that the well-born ranks of the Senate were grudgingly opened to a mere talent. Small wonder that Cicero's susceptible nature was on fire. Born orator, he was part actor, needed an audience, and throve on applause. It was natural to him to think that other people watched him.

Politically, Sulla was an extreme conservative. His dictatorship had been devoted to restoring a constitution which had already proved inadequate to rule an empire. At home, it was full of legal checks and balances intended to prevent any one man from getting too strong. Abroad, however, the rule of a governor in his province or of a general in the field was absolute. Naturally governors plundered shamelessly, using their money when they got home to buy themselves influence.

Roman magistrates might belong to the great families, but their election to the regular ladder of offices depended on the people. The character of the people, however, was rapidly changing. Citizenship had recently been granted to all Italians and was automatically the possession of the freed slave of any Roman. The proletariat was therefore becoming mixed, and the greatest addition had been to the ranks of the unemployed poor. The growth of slavery had taken the bread out of the mouth of the working-class man, with the result that increasing numbers of Romans lived hand-to-mouth, forming gangs hired by politicians, and frankly selling their votes. For this reason, it was becoming expensive to stand for election. People beggared themselves to do so. Then, since magistracy in Rome was regularly followed by a term of office abroad, they recouped their finances from the unfortunate provinces they governed.

On this shameful process, new men like Cicero looked with indignation. They belonged almost entirely to the middle-class ranks of the state, and were known as the Knights. Anyone not a Senator and having a certain minimum wealth could call himself a Knight. Their interests were tightly bound together by the fact that a Senator might not engage in trade. As a result, all the great corporations which imperial expansion produced, even including those of the tax gatherers, were in the hands of the Knights. Naturally they had their political lobbies and Senators attached to their interests. In fact, the party of Marius had been linked with the Knights, who had resented their exclusion from the perquisites of office.

Business morality being what it always has been, there was very little to choose between the Knightly and the Senatorial groups in the matter of corruption. There was, however, a good deal to be said for letting each check on the other. The terrible scandals of the late Republic tend to blind us to the fact that there were men of goodwill who resisted the temptations of easy money. These thought in terms of controlling the evil by a series of prudent measures, while preserving the traditional forms of the Roman Republic.

In such a group, Cicero was a natural leader, marked out by his talents, by his fresh view as a new man, and by his real goodness, which even his later enemies respected. The years following Sulla's death were years of growing opposition to unchallenged Senatorial rule. A liberal party of sorts was being patched together, including many with private interests at heart. Among these Cicero stands out, not because his political methods are superior to theirs but because he looks for no gain except in reputation. His greatest achievement at this time was his sensational exposure of the governorship of Caius Verres in Sicily.

This was another case like that of Roscius, so scandalous that when the facts were brought out, even authorities had no defense to make. Verres was one of those dreadful Romans of whom Nero is a notorious example. His eating, his drinking, his debauchery were shameless. His greed was insatiable, his selfishness complete. He was lazy, covetous, and cruel. He devoted such energies as he had to one thing only, to extracting wealth from the Sicilians, not refraining from murder and every form of injustice to do it. He retired from his governorship literally gorged with plunder, much consisting in priceless works of Greek art. For Verres, like Nero and Göring, had taste in these things. It is a comfort to learn that he was eventually murdered at the instance of Mark Antony, who also had an eye for art and coveted his collection.

If the case was notorious, however, it was not easy for Cicero to marshal the facts. Provincials were naturally frightened to talk and most reluctant to give evidence in a Roman court. Many Senators who may personally have been contemptuous of Verres were anxious to cover up his misdeeds at all costs. There was an agitation on foot to get the juries which normally tried such cases transferred from the Senate to the Knights. This would, the Senate maintained, reduce all governors to servants of the great moneylenders and tax-collecting firms. This was, they contended, as undesirable as an occasional Verres.

For these reasons, Cicero had a difficult task. So devastating, however, was his opening blast that Verres did not wait for the rest. He fled into exile, leaving Cicero to publish the vast indictment he would have delivered. This is not merely crushing; it is almost incredible. It must even have struck his contemporaries with horrified wonder that such things could possibly be. Cicero did not mince words. Master of a magnificent talent for vituperation, he lived at a period when speech was not controlled by laws of libel. Fearless of consequences, he spoke to hurt. Such talents are dangerous to possess. He would pay for them later.

Cicero was now in his late thirties, unchallenged head of the Roman bar and foremost orator on the political scene. He had married a dominating lady whom he speaks of with respect. Affectionate and impulsive, Cicero might seem cut out for domestic life; but a Roman marriage was usually a business arrangement. His heart's darling was his daughter Tullia, while his pride was little Marcus, born in 67 B.C. Apart from his children, his brother held first place in his life. Quintus, much less able, suffered from the comparison between them. Marcus, flashing with ideas and scintillating with wit, was an elder brother whose very affection might seem dominating. Quintus's temper made relations a difficulty, and yet the brothers were devoted.

In two cases of friendship, Cicero received far more. By his servants he was always beloved, but with Tiro, his secretary, his relation went far beyond that of mere master and slave. Similarly with Atticus, his best friend, his confidence was unreserved. The character of Atticus was a pleasant foil to his own. While Cicero was indiscreet, careless with money, up and down in temperament, Atticus was cautious and sensible. Politics to Cicero were the breath of life, while Atticus held himself aloof. Thus Cicero would write or speak as he felt, leaving Atticus to be calm, impartial, and wise. Their lifelong intimacy was never clouded.

With his rivals or partners on the political scene, Cicero's relations were less close. It is true, he was liked and admired in spite of his sharp tongue. His culture was very great, his conversation witty, and his character noble. Notwithstanding, he was not like a true-born aristocrat; and many an eyebrow must have been raised with a hint of condescension. He was too voluble, too much of an actor. One perceived his demand for admiration. "Look at me," he seemed to be saying. "Look where I have got to!" As his position consolidated itself, these exclamations became less brash; but they did not cease to exist. They were a matter of temperament and style, not really detracting from his good sense or wisdom; but they managed to underline his newness.

In his forties, Cicero settled down. His own position was assured, while the reactionary parts of Sulla's constitution had now been swept away. It would have been possible for Cicero to strike out a political line of his own, if he had had one. Surprisingly, it began to be clear he had not. Temperamentally, he was a conservative, entirely devoted to the high ideals of the ancient Roman Republic. Even on questions where he might well have had advanced views, he was strangely silent. In 63, for instance, he became the first newcomer to hold the consulship since Marius, a generation before. He noted the fact with intense pride, but it never led him to suggest it was time that the Senate admitted fresh talent. None of Cicero's efforts were truly directed toward reform. What he wanted was to restore the State, not to change it.

It is easy from our much longer view to pronounce him shortsighted. From that of his own day, it is fairer to call him a patriot, in love with Rome as he saw her and yet anxious to raise the standards of public life. He was, however, also a politician and willing to make the deals that go with that profession. For however important and respected he might be, in politics he was lightweight. This must have been obvious to him, and it stemmed from three factors over which he had no control. As a new man, he had not the relationships and marriage connections which bound his rivals together. He was not a general, and he was not rich. He had therefore no army with which to threaten the Senate and no money with which to hire street gangs. Respect and influence he might acquire, but he lacked naked power.

This being the case, what Cicero desperately needed was a powerful ally of similar views. His personal ideal was what he called the "harmony of the orders"; that is, the old Republic of plebeians, Senators, and Knights, each serving the State in its appointed way, and none presuming to dominate the rest. Unfortunately, in Cicero's day the old Republic could hardly be maintained without the backing of generals powerful enough to overturn it. The new armies of Marius had done their work. Cicero, however, was a natural optimist; and the appeal of patriotism was strong. Indeed, it happened that a general did lie ready to Cicero's hand with views and qualities which suited his purpose.

Cnaius Pompey, or Pompey the Great, as he liked to be called, was Cicero's own age — in other words, twenty-eight when Sulla had died. In spite of this, however, he had already risen to be one of Sulla's lieutenants. Sulla had not only used him extensively in command, but he had allowed him to break the careful rules which prevented people from becoming prominent early. Thus when Sulla died, Pompey was already in a position to aspire to dictatorship if he wished. It soon became clear that he did not. What Pompey wanted was to be an exception to all the rules which were made for other people, to become, for instance, consul without ever being a junior magistrate. He wanted to command the Republic's armies, fight its battles, and tell it now and then what it ought to do. He liked the Senators to throng his anterooms and ask his opinion, yet he was contented to leave the government in other hands.

In the circumstances, perhaps, no safer general than Pompey could be found to handle the Republic's armies. Cicero certainly thought so, and the alliance between these two in the sixties became very close. Cicero lent his eloquence to two important laws entrusting vast problems to Pompey. The first of these was the task of putting down piracy. Civil war, exile, and anarchy had filled the Mediterranean with pirates. Yet when a governor of some harried province attempted to stamp out the evil, the pirates merely shifted their home bases elsewhere. What was needed was a wide, all-embracing command, which was exactly the sort of thing that the Roman Republic was jealous of granting. Pompey, however, was appointed with Cicero's aid and swept the seas.

The second task was on a still larger scale. Roman misgovernment had brought about a revolt in what we now describe as Turkey and parts of the Middle East. A native king, Mithridates of Pontus, had swept over the area, massacring Romans on a large scale and throwing several provinces into confusion. This was again a matter which could not be tackled piecemeal. The whole organization of the Middle East was at stake. Dependent kingdoms which had taken this side or that would need to be dealt with. Frontiers would have to be redrawn, whole territories annexed, new treaties drawn up. In short, someone or other would have to settle the affairs of the East as far as the Euphrates.

Perhaps no one but Pompey, after deciding the fate of kings and peoples, would have been willing to come back to Rome as a private man. In this sense Cicero was not mistaken in him. Yet Pompey's private rank was a mockery thereafter. He had but to show himself in the East to raise the world in arms. He needed only to call his old soldiers to action without stirring from his place in Rome, and there would have been civil war. Pompey knew this; and so did the Senate, which unwisely tried to cut him down to size. The truth of the matter was that imperial tasks were already on too big a scale for private persons. Cicero's influence and the character of Pompey himself might put off a crisis, yet sooner or later it must come.

Dedicated to the task of rejuvenating the Republic, Cicero could not remain unaware that other people were as anxious to tear it down. Some of these might be genuine reformers convinced that the old pattern did not fit the new times. Others of them, however, were clearly adventurers. The vicious system of buying popular votes in Rome had bankrupted many. Extravagant habits and a lack of occupation, particularly for young aristocrats, plunged others into debt. Revolution presented itself to such men as a chance for plunder, while among the loose and shiftless population of Rome there were plenty to follow their lead. It became evident that a radical party was being formed under the leadership of Lucius Catiline, who stood for the consulship for 63 with the avowed intention of introducing revolutionary measures.

Sixty-three happened also to be the year in which Cicero was qualified to hold the consulship. It was the great desire of his life to be consul, to have risen from Arpinum to the top, as Marius had done. All his efforts were devoted to obtaining this coveted prize.

He was not rich enough, to buy votes, but he had friends with influence. It was not the custom for an advocate to take a fee at the Roman bar, but naturally when Cicero won a case he both expected and received some sort of service. By this time a great many people owed him favors. Those who did not were terrified lest Catiline get in, and they threw their weight on Cicero's side. The tactic was successful. Cicero and a third candidate, Caius Antonius, were elected.

Caius Antonius was a man of straw, supposed to favor

Catiline in a mild way. Cicero immediately gained his goodwill by resigning to him a proconsular appointment to the
rich province of Macedonia, which was to follow their consulship. Cicero did not want a province himself, preferring
Rome and being uninterested in absolute power or illegal
wealth. He was thus enabled at no sacrifice to have the administration of Rome for a whole year at his discretion.

Catiline, meanwhile, was desperate. He had not the financial resources to try for the consulship over and over again.
No other alternative to ruin presented itself except revolution. Hastily, he began to plan revolt while he still commanded a show of wealth and influence. Here, however, he
alienated some of his previous backers, who were indeed
anxious to put through radical changes but regarded armed
revolution as irresponsible. The thing began therefore to be
whispered about, and presently the consul was warned.

Catiline, it seemed, had reckoned without Cicero, who
might be no soldier and was thought to be personally timid.
All the same he had quick wits and moral courage. Timing
his action perfectly, he attacked Catiline in a brilliant speech
as the conspirator paid his last visit to the Senate before
leaving in secret to set up his standard. Simultaneously,
orders were sent out to call up levies, and men were set in
command. Undetected, however, there remained a group in
Rome still planning a supplementary coup. These leaders,
five in number, were unmasked by the consul and arrested.
The Senate, now terribly alarmed lest the ramifications of
the conspiracy extend further yet, held a momentous debate.
Should they execute the five at once and take the heart out

of the revolt? It was illegal to put a citizen to death without trial, but the emergency was great. The guilt of the accused had been established by letters in their own hands and by their confessions. Cicero as consul stated he was willing to order execution if the Senate would pass a decree empowering him to do so.

Thus exhorted, the Senate got up its courage. Cicero acted, and the effect was salutary indeed. Catiline's army began to melt away and was easily scattered. What might have been a bloody revolution had been averted by the decisive actions of the consul.

This was the proudest moment of Cicero's life. He had saved the State he loved and had also shown himself as prompt as those who called themselves men of action. Perhaps he had even surprised himself on this occasion, for he never allowed anyone to forget it. He even wrote a long poem on his own consulship, most of which has unhappily vanished except for one crashing line of self-admiration: "Oh lucky Rome that I was consul then!"

It is a pity that we do not have the rest, for the ridiculous side of Cicero makes him human. People laughed at him in his own day, and yet this never interfered with the love they bore him for qualities he also possessed.

The death of Catiline merely cleared the way for a pair of politicians who were far more dangerous. Marcus Crassus, the richest man in Rome, was the natural representative in the Senate of the Knights. In politics, wealth counted. The power of Crassus was very difficult to measure, since a great deal of it was secret. Nevertheless, it clearly existed, attracting to itself the same sort of people as had in an earlier generation followed Marius. Many were only anxious to cut themselves a slice of political cake, yet even their self-seeking was based on a clear understanding that the forms of the old Republic no longer worked.

Crassus himself was a Senator, so that his financial empire was delegated, more or less under cover. His wide interests were well known, and yet on a formal basis he did not engage in trade. Similarly, he did not hand out the bribes or make the deals on which his political power was based, except just possibly at the very highest level. He entrusted that part of the business to Julius Caesar, a very wily politician, whose dangerous abilities were just beginning to be understood. Caesar and Crassus were frankly out for power. What they would do with it when they got it remained to be seen. Meanwhile, however, they were prepared to stoop to dubious methods.

The crisis came to a head in the year 59. This was Caesar's year to be consul if elected. It was therefore his chance. Far more able than Crassus, he had no intention of remaining subordinate to him. He saw, moreover, that without a great military power at his back he would never be a rival to Pompey. During Cicero's consulship, Pompey had been absent in the East. A year or two later he returned, and Rome held its breath. What would he do, this man who had made kings? What position would he demand in the State? To the astonishment of most and the relief of many, Pompey laid down his power, disbanded his army, and retired into private life.

Pompey so far had justified Cicero's confidence in him,

yet the matter could not rest there. The Senate still feared him, and Pompey was still vain. His promise to his veterans of severance pay demanded a law, which the Senate short-sightedly rejected. This was trying Pompey too high. It was something he could not afford to put up with, since his position depended on the goodwill of his men. Without it, he might even come to be in danger. He certainly would lose enormous prestige.

In this situation, Caesar saw a chance to detach Pompey from the conservatives and use him for his own ends. A combination of the influences of Pompey and Crassus would certainly suffice to elect Caesar as consul. Once in, he would use his position to pass Pompey's law, together with a financial measure which Crassus wanted. For himself, he would put through a law assigning to him command of the province of Gaul for five years with an army. At this time Rome possessed a province on the south coast of Gaul, which is still called Provence. Due to the weakness of the Gallic tribes in the interior, the whole of Gaul was threatened by invasion from migrating nations, mainly German. The dangers to Provence were great, and it was clear that war impended on what might be a big scale. To counterbalance the tremendous eastern powers of Pompey, this situation in Gaul was not impressive. It was there, however, and it was a chance. Caesar wanted to grab it.

Lawmaking at this time was chiefly in the hands of the Senate. It was, however, legal for the consul to propose and carry laws in the assembly of the people. All the same, the checks and balances of the Roman system made this operation a difficult one. There were, for instance ten tribunes, each with power of veto. Since all magistrates came from the aristocratic group, it naturally followed that some of the tribunes would be bound to hold with the Senate. These would veto Caesar's laws. It is true that tribunes might be beaten up or threatened. Great, however, as the power of Crassus was, he did not control every tough in Rome. An obstinate tribune could certainly find the means of guarding himself. Faced with this situation, Caesar threw discretion to the winds. He passed his laws, ignoring the tribunes' veto and every other legal check the Senate discovered. It was vain for conservatives to protest that such laws were not valid. Caesar was the chief executive and in a position to put them into operation.

So far Caesar's affairs had prospered, but in politics one has to take a long view. What would happen if he went to Gaul for five years, leaving behind him an angry Senate perfectly determined to bring him to trial the moment he came home? To be sure, he might then have an army; but his alliance with Pompey would probably be dissolved. Crassus, too, might have decided to throw him over. Five years in any case would give his enemies a chance to rally under leadership.

Chief of these enemies was Cicero. Caesar's illegal methods were an outrage to his whole conception of the State. Besides, every one of these important measures which Caesar had put through was a personal favor to someone who wanted power. They had no relationship to decent government or principle. Now Cicero, though by no means

powerful himself, was highly influential. His eloquence
swayed men. His consulship had made him respected by people who before might have thought him wordy and lacking
in the qualities for action. In fact, given time, Cicero could
be dangerous. Caesar saw this and determined that before
he left Rome, Cicero must be dealt with.

Curiously enough, Caesar and Cicero had more in common than any other two politicians of the age. They were,
for one thing, both geniuses. Caesar's was the more practical
one, yet he possessed in a fair measure nearly all the gifts of
Cicero himself. He also was a man of very wide culture, an
orator, the possessor of considerable literary gifts. Both of
them were witty men, fascinating in conversation, the posses-
sors of soaring imaginations. Finally Caesar, despite the un-
scrupulousness of his methods, was also in his own way a
patriot. He intended to use his power in the service of Rome
when he got it. For all these reasons, he really loved Cicero
and spared no effort to detach him from his conservative
friends. Had he not started his career as a liberal? Could he
not be persuaded that Caesar himself intended reform?
What did Cicero want? The alliance of the Triumvirs, or the
Three, as they were called, would have been more welcome
to Caesar himself if it had been Four. Cicero and Pompey
were old friends, too. Every form of temptation was tried.
Cicero was flattered. Caesar was lavish of his own great personal charm. It was all no good. Cicero was simply too great
a man to be tempted by such inducements.

This being the case, Cicero must be dealt with. After his
consulship, Caesar moved to the outskirts of Rome for the

simple reason that he could not assume his proconsular office inside the city. If, however, he delayed doing so for a single day, he became automatically a private man and would have been arrested. He did not immediately set out for his province. He waited while a tribune in his pay attacked Cicero.

Publius Clodius was a dissolute young man who a short time earlier had created a nasty scandal by disguising himself as a woman to take part in some very private rites performed officially by the wives of leading men on behalf of the city. Sacrilege being involved, the matter was serious. Clodius with bare-faced effrontery put forward an alibi. This, however, was broken by Cicero, who happened to have met him in Rome, whereas he claimed that he was elsewhere. In the event, Crassus and Caesar decided Clodius would be useful to them and bought his acquittal by tremendous bribes to the jury. He was, however, a deadly enemy of Cicero thenceforward.

This Clodius now brought forward a bill to the assembly condemning to exile any man who had put a citizen to death without trial. The measure was aimed expressly at Cicero for the acts of his consulship, even though the Senate had passed an enabling bill before the execution of the Catiline conspirators. Clodius, subsidized by Crassus, controlled the street gangs, and passage of the measure seemed quite certain.

Cicero was desperate. This was ruin. This was the end. Rome was the whole of his life. He had no other and did not care to make one. Useless to appeal to Crassus, with whom he had never been on good terms. But what about Pompey? Were they not friends?

They were indeed, and Pompey's position in the matter was most undignified. To do him justice, he had tried to explain to his colleagues that he could make Cicero hold his tongue. By now, however, it was clear that he could not. Pompey's own interests bound him to support the acts of Caesar. The best thing he could think of was to retire to the country, pretending to take no part in political matters, while in fact his influence supported Clodius. The bill was passed, and Cicero was driven into exile.

It was a crushing blow, and he saw no reason to bear it with dignity. It was his nature to be up or down. In his letters he simply poured out his feelings. No one ever had suffered such a fall or been the victim of such a terrible injustice. He should have fallen on his sword. Indeed, it would probably come to that in the end, but the moment for doing so with honor had been lost. His friends had failed him, or else had counseled him wrong. He wallowed in depression.

As a matter of fact, his exile lasted only a year and a half. Caesar was not vindictive. As soon as Cicero perceived his powerlessness and was in a mood to be persuaded that he could not attack the Triumvirs, Caesar was anxious to have him recalled. He even offered a place on his staff to Quintus Cicero, a valuable appointment which gave Marcus much more pleasure than a favor done to himself. Clodius, of course, was irreconcilable and still tyrannizing over the Roman streets. A rival, however, aided by some of Cicero's friends, had actually hired a band of gladiators and with them fought Clodius to a standstill. To such a low point had Republican politics sunk! Cicero, returning, could only make the best of a bad job.

From this time on, Cicero was practically powerless. Caesar's command in Gaul was extended to ten years, and his startling victories made it evident that a new power had arisen, comparable to Pompey's. Cicero had to make the best of this. The task was easier because Caesar spared no pains to win his friendship. His treatment of Quintus was distinguished. Any favor which he could do Cicero was performed. His letters were couched in flattering, intimate terms. In these circumstances, the natural affinity between the two men had a chance to do its work. They liked each other and in a sense spoke the same language. Cicero was trying to believe that after all, Julius Caesar was just another Pompey. After his triumph, he would lay down his powers like a loyal son of the Republic.

Meanwhile, his own affairs were becoming involved. At the time of his exile, his house had been destroyed by the mob. Never prudent in money matters, he now was troubled by cares for which he was unfitted. His relation with Terentia, his wife, was heading for divorce. Life was driving him, as it were, inward. Constantly frustrated in politics and private life, he turned to literature.

Cicero's literary compositions in form resemble Plato's. That is to say, they are dialogues in which a group of characters discuss a subject, such as rhetoric, the ideal commonwealth, or law. As might be expected, they show charm and intelligence. They are the product of a brilliant man who has not, however, a great original mind. Cicero is in effect translating the best of Greek culture into Roman thoughts and modern terms. His own contribution is from experience rather than to theory. Notwithstanding, they mark him as a great literary figure and have kept their popularity through the ages.

In 51, much against his will he had to take charge of a province. Such an office came usually after the consulship, and Cicero had been at pains to avoid it then. On this occasion he took it with reluctance, but displayed himself a model governor, refusing not merely bribes but official receptions which cost money. Never a military man, he yet conducted a small successful border campaign with the help of his brother, fresh from his military experiences with Caesar. It was a very minor affair, as he freely admitted; but his troops saluted him as "Imperator." This raised the question of a Roman triumph, and the temptation was too much for his vanity. What a crown for his success! He became excited over the prospect and nearly attained it. On returning, however, he found it swept away by greater issues.

It had been evident for some time that Caesar and Pompey were going to dispute the mastery of the world. Given, however, the curious character of Pompey, now the servant, now the master of the state, the form of the conflict had seemed uncertain. It now at last became obvious that there would be civil war, and people were taking sides. Justifiably from their own point of view, the Senatorial party was unanimously for Pompey, whom they had managed more or less for many years. Cicero's allegiance was equally certain, but his friendship with Caesar and his absence from the center of things during the last year had allowed him to hope that all might be patched up. When hostilities did break out, his loyalty to Pompey was strong. His position, however, was not an easy one.

Pompey's strength lay in Spain and the East, Caesar's in Gaul and northern Italy. It was necessary, therefore, for Pompey to abandon Rome and betake himself to one end or the other of the Mediterranean. Cicero, who was nearly sixty by now, was not much use to him in a military camp, despite his recent exhibition of generalship. He hesitated, wooed by Caesar with flattering letters and hoping against hope that he might mediate between them. By the time he had actually decided that his duty lay with Pompey, it was not easy to leave Italy at all, while the fortunes of the Republicans already looked black. Disdaining to wait and see what happened, Cicero escaped to northern Greece, where Pompey was. In the actual campaign between the two great generals, he took no part. Having made it clear on which side he belonged, he could do no more. When Pompey was at last defeated and killed, there was nothing for it but to go back to Italy.

He arrived at Brundisium in a state of deep depression and was forced to wait there for nearly a year until Caesar decided what he was going to do with him. In truth, Caesar's intentions were of the kindest, but he was busy in Egypt and elsewhere. There was no way for Cicero to guess at his intentions. Either the climate of Brundisium or else his recent travels had upset his health. His relations with his wife were worse than ever. His dear daughter was unhappily married. The Republic lay in ruins. The fate of Quintus, who had also joined the Republican side, was on his mind. Sunk in depression, he was even resigned to face his execution.

There was of course no question of such a thing. When Caesar finally arrived in Italy and Cicero, perforce, went to meet him, the victorious general jumped off his horse, as eager for friendship as he had ever been. Of course Cicero would return to Rome and his old position. Must they not all of them join to restore the state to its old glory?

Cicero tried, but it did not work. The truth was, Caesar's solution to the urgent problems of Rome differed widely from the old Republican ideal. This became clearer and clearer. Dictatorship, even a remarkably magnanimous one, was not an atmosphere in which Cicero could breathe. Besides, his private troubles grew worse. He did finally put through a divorce and marry again, but the arrangement — another business one — was not happy. The crushing blow was the death of Tullia. Young Marcus, who later developed into the deepest drinker in the social world of imperial Rome, was not at this point an unsatisfactory son. Yet, no doubt about it, his was a commonplace nature compared to his father's. Little Tullia was Cicero's darling, and now he had lost her.

He made the best of things, wrote several more dialogues, appeared in the defense of some Pompeians, interceded with Caesar for others, and watched bitterly the destruction of his hopes. The old Republic was daily being torn down, and not restored.

The murder of Caesar in March, 44 B.C., was an electrifying event in Roman politics, not so much because it happened as because people of the caliber of Cicero approved of it. Nothing illustrates more plainly the terrible bitterness of the old-style patriot at this time. The whole tendency of Cicero's life was against such an act. He had no share in it and did not desire one. He had even liked Caesar as a person. Notwithstanding, he gloried in the deed. Many dangers no doubt lay ahead, but it was possible that freedom might be restored.

The dangers were not slow in mounting. Mark Antony, Caesar's chief lieutenant, was unscrupulous and greedy. The conspirators were indecisive. Not having behind them an armed force such as Antony had, they were uncertain how to capitalize on what seemed general public rejoicing. In the event, they fled to Greece to raise an army. Antony, a far worse master than Caesar, took possession of Rome. It was obvious that things would go from bad to worse in his hands. At this moment, and in the nick of time, another claimant to Caesar's power turned up, the young Octavian, Caesar's eighteen-year-old great-nephew and heir, an unknown quantity.

Antony, of course, simply laughed the boy off; but young Octavian proved to have a mind of his own. He made advances to Caesar's soldiers, not all of whom were under Antony's direct control. In addition, he approached the conserv-

atives of the Senate, headed by Cicero. These were now
ready to grasp at any straw which might save them from the
intolerable Antony. Octavian, young enough to be influenced, deferring readily to Cicero's wisdom and fame,
seemed such an instrument. Might he not under guidance
turn out to be another Pompey? It seemed possible. Girding
himself for the conflict, Cicero dashed into his last battle.

It was a desperate risk, and he must have known it. It is
true that Antony was forced to leave Rome to deal with the
adherents of Brutus and Cassius. All the governors of all the
provinces, each with his army, were rapidly taking sides. It
was impossible for Antony to linger in Rome at such a moment.

But though Antony left Rome, restoring brief freedom of
action to Cicero and the Senate, he still looked considerably
stronger than Brutus and Cassius or Octavian. Besides, these
two forces, on opposite sides of the fence, were only
vaguely in communication. How could Octavian combine
with the murderers of his adopted father?

Such considerations were all very true, but now was the
moment to speak out for what one felt right. The death knell
of the Republic had not quite sounded yet, and it was possible that a clear call to arms might save it. Who should utter
this but the greatest orator in the world? Who else could do
justice to the subject?

The fruits of this situation were twelve orations of Cicero,
known in imitation of a famous Greek model as his Philippics. Seldom has anyone risen more splendidly to an occasion. In form they are speeches against Antony, employing

all Cicero's marvelous talents in vituperation. He is abusive, sarcastic, disgusted, contemptuous, angry by turns. He spares neither Antony's character, his personal habits, his appearance, his ancestry, history, ethics, political actions, nor anything that is his. He exposes him, naked and loathsome, before the eyes of people with whom he had worked and grown up. And if only half of what he said was true, Antony was horrible.

Such was the effect of the Philippics, yet abuse of Antony was only a part of Cicero's task, and the least important. The purpose of the speeches was to save the Republic, to set an example, to call on others to follow a clear lead. Seldom has freedom been defended with such power — and all of it wasted, for the Republic was dead. The young Octavian, who was to have been its champion, had no intention of espousing the cause of Brutus and Cassius. As soon as, with Cicero's support and by his own efforts, he had attained a position of power, he marched against Antony and made a deal. Three men would split the world, Octavian, Antony, and a minor partner called Lepidus, who happened to be in command of an important province. As a preliminary to taking hold, they planned a purge.

The proscription lists now drawn up by Antony, Octavian, and Lepidus make those of Sulla look almost childish. The principle they went on was that if any one of them desired a man's death, be it for a trivial reason, he should be allowed to have his way. It was on this occasion, for instance, that Antony inserted the name of Verres for the sake of his art treasures. One single exception, or so legend has it, was made to this general rule. For three days Antony and Octavian wrangled about the life of Cicero. He was now an old man, after all, and a very great one. Octavian admired him. Besides, he had shot his bolt. But Antony was adamant, and in the circumstances one can hardly wonder. No man who had written the Philippics could have expected to live.

The end came quickly after that. There were terrible scenes of panic as everybody sought hiding. Quintus Cicero and his son were on the list. They died bravely. Marcus was in his country villa at the time and was disposed to wait for the assassins who he knew would be sent to hunt him down. Why should he go into exile again? This was his country, and he would rather die in it. His servants, however, implored him to escape. At last he yielded to them and set out, but he only traveled to another villa he had near the sea. He was sixty-three, an old man by Roman standards; and his health had not recovered. Soon pursuers were heard of in the neighborhood. His slaves bundled him into a litter and tried to rush rapidly down rocky paths to a waiting boat. They were too late. Presently the noise of pursuit was heard behind. His servants clustered round him, prepared to die in his defence; but he forbade them to sacrifice themselves. So they set the litter on the ground and Cicero waited, resting his chin on his hand as he often did.

Thus died Cicero, his final effort as glorious as it was useless. For in the judgment of posterity, it is always worthwhile to speak for freedom in a crisis. Something perished in Cicero's day which had real value, even though the empire of the Romans benefited by the change. There is a legend extant which gives Cicero a fitting epitaph.

A generation later, Plutarch says, the emperor Augustus, who had once been the young Octavian, was walking in his garden when he came upon one of the princes of his house who was reading Cicero. The boy tried to escape, but he was fairly caught. Augustus took the roll out of his hands and studied it in a rather awful silence. Considering how Cicero had died and Octavian's share in it, it was natural that his name was not mentioned in the imperial household. The boy, therefore, waited in terror, holding his breath. But after some moments, Augustus gave him back the roll, merely remarking, "A man of great abilities, my child, and one who loved his country."

CAESAR

Caius Julius Caesar, 102–44 B.C.

CAESAR was born in 102, just about at the climax of the great career of Caius Marius, which was fated to have even more effect on Caesar's future than it did on Cicero's. For Julia, Marius's wife, was Caesar's aunt. Roman alliances being calculated things, it followed that Caesar was from his earliest years marked out by his connections as a prominent person in the Marian party.

This situation seems to have been unwelcome to his father. The Julian clan was ancient and aristocratic, actually claiming descent from the goddess Venus through Aeneas, a legendary hero of Troy who escaped from the sack of the city. The family of the Caesars, which had appeared in history during the third century B.C., had taken an honorable, though not especially distinguished part in Roman affairs. Now, unexpectedly, it had allied itself with a newcomer of low birth and should presumably have risen through his influence. Yet the elder Caesar, though he held the praetorship, retired early from public life. His wife, Aurelia, meanwhile, had two brothers who were prominent among the supporters of Sulla.

Since he was well connected on either side, it should have been possible for the elder Caesar to increase the influence of his son in similar fashion. Surprisingly, however, he married his daughter to a rich Italian and arranged an engagement between young Caesar and a girl of wealth but quite obscure connections. At this point he died suddenly, when his son was about eighteen. Caesar's mother, Aurelia, whom he seems to have much resembled, was far more ambitious. The engagement was soon broken off. A little while later Caesar married Cornelia, daughter of Cinna, who had succeeded Marius as leader of his party.

At the time this match was made, Cinna ruled in Rome, while Sulla was occupied with a war in the East. About a year later, Sulla and his victorious army returned to drive the Marians out and massacre them. Caesar was now in a dangerous position. He was only twenty, to be sure, and personally unimportant, while his father had taken no share in events and left no enemies. All the same, he was first cousin of the younger Marius, whom Sulla had put to death. He was also husband of Cinna's daughter. Sulla demanded that he divorce her. It must be remembered that Roman divorce was easy enough. It merely consisted of sending a wife back home and returning her dowry. But Caesar refused it.

This was too much for Sulla, who confiscated the dowry and added Caesar's name to the proscription lists. The young man fled into hiding in the wild Apennine country, constantly traveling from place to place one jump ahead of pursuers. Indeed, the story goes that he was actually caught and only talked himself out of death by offering money which he had ready to hand, pointing out that it would be easier to collect than the reward promised by the government. At all events, he escaped; but his life was a hard one. He caught malaria and had to be hurried from place to place on a litter.

Meanwhile, Aurelia had been at work. She had great influence through her brothers and other connections, so that eventually she managed to extract a pardon. Since, however, it was clearly not safe in Rome, Caesar went abroad. Unlike Cicero in similar circumstances, he did not study, but made straight for the army, serving with minor distinction in two campaigns and being chosen to negotiate with a local king, Nicholas of Bithynia, with whom he struck up a friendship. Thus by the time Sulla died, he had already seen a good deal of the East and had gained understanding of how the Empire looked to non-Roman eyes.

In 78, he returned to Rome and lost no time in attacking the conservative party, as Cicero did, through the law courts. He was unsuccessful, however, partly because he was not willing to wait for a favorable moment. The aristocratic party closed ranks to support notorious offenders. In addition, Caesar had neither Cicero's supreme talents nor his training. Well educated and with natural gifts as a speaker, he was yet no match for the leaders of the Roman bar. He soon perceived this and went to Rhodes, as Cicero had done, for further study. He was not, however, destined to spend much time with Cicero's master. On his way over, he was captured by pirates.

The pirates of the Mediterranean recruited their numbers

almost openly from gangs in the coastal cities. A pirate in his home port looks like anyone else; and it was not easy to exterminate them, more especially since many of the towns-people shared in their profits. It was, however, intolerable that Romans should be captured on the high seas and held to ransom. For this reason, coastal cities were forced to put up the ransom for Roman citizens. This ensured that the presence of pirates in their seas should be expensive. Since, however, a great deal of the booty was not Roman, pirates still prospered.

Caesar's ransom was fixed at fifty talents, a very large sum. To himself, the amount did not matter. He sent those that were with him away to collect it, while remaining as a hostage with the pirates. These were rough and desperate people, no less bloody than pirates have always been. Caesar, though he represented a big ransom, was in constant danger of being brutally treated or murdered out of caprice. Legend says that he behaved with the utmost coolness, joining quite gaily in their life, and even joking about how he would come back and capture them all and put them to death as they deserved.

Everybody laughed at that, including Caesar. After about a month, however, the ransom arrived. The pirates let Caesar go, and they started celebrating. He, meanwhile, made his way at once to Miletus, where he persuaded crews to enlist with him for the sake of the fifty talents and other plunder. With these improvised forces he fell on the roistering pirates, captured them, and put them all to death, just as he had promised.

The tale seems true in the main, if not in detail. It gives us, moreover, an interesting picture of what the ancient world thought about Caesar. His biographers sound faintly shocked that he should have been able to hunt down personally a group which may have deserved it, but with whom he had for a while been almost friendly. Conceding qualities of leadership and personal courage, they find him cold-blooded. And it is true that Caesar had a capacity for cool judgment which had nothing to do with his feelings. He was personally charming, devoted to his friends, did not even bear malice against those who had wronged him. Yet if he decided that the time had come to be stern, no prayers would move him. It is in this quality, perhaps, that his genius consists. He saw more clearly than his contemporaries and could act on his vision. It is also his weakness, however. Caesar made enemies because he did not respect other people's feelings.

Back in Rome by 74, Caesar settled down to the regular series of elected magistracies topped by the consulate and varied by periods of service in a province. By itself, this could bring him a distinguished career, yet not a great one. The prospect was not enough for Caesar's ambition. Personal power had become the aim of every would-be great man, of whom there were many in the Roman state. Caesar differed from the others only in a clearer insight into what he could accomplish with it.

If he wanted power, how could he get it? The proscriptions of Sulla had been so effective that an opposition hardly existed inside the magic circle to which Caesar himself belonged. Commands abroad or offices at home were in the hands of men who looked upon Caesar, though one of themselves, as suspect. In this situation, it would be necessary for him to advance in despite of his colleagues, rather than through them. The achievement would not be easy, but Caesar brought to it marvelous political gifts and lack of scruples.

He set out in the first place to captivate social Rome. He was no great winer and diner, partly because he liked to keep fit, but apparently also because his health was not strong. The malaria caught in the Apennines troubled him for years, while at some later time, perhaps in his forties, he became subject to epileptic fits. These cannot have been frequent, considering his later physical achievements; but they reinforce a pattern on which all writers agree. Caesar was slender, wiry, something of an athlete and a notable horseman. He was capable of enduring great fatigue; and yet in general, his health was a care to him from youth. He was not really strong.

If he was not a performer at Roman dinners, Caesar had social qualities of his own. Highly intelligent, witty in conversation, he was a great ladies' man. Aurelia knew all the leading ladies in a rather brilliant set. Caesar, who lived with his mother on very intimate terms, knew them likewise and soon broadened his acquaintance to include those of his own age. Young Roman matrons of the time had a great deal of freedom. Flirtations, even scandals were commonplace. True or untrue, much was soon whispered about Caesar which gave the impression to his contemporaries that he was essentially a trivial man. The pretense was useful, and he reinforced it by great attention to dress. The stripe on his toga was broader than other people's. His fringes were wider. His girdle was looser. He was meticulously shaven, perfumed, and polished. When early baldness overtook him, he made tremendous efforts to cover it up by arranging his hair over the top of his head. Even Cicero, acuter than most, made the comment that a man who would take pains over such an object was little to be feared.

His formidable talents could not be entirely concealed. As a public speaker, he soon ranked among the best. His literary skill was early evident in verse and prose. His broader studies included astronomy and ancient maps. He was interested to a remarkable degree for his times in the non-Roman world. Since, however, his qualities in action were not understood in Rome, he passed on the whole for a dilettante. Only gradually did it come to be whispered that half the more radical troubles of the time had Caesar at bottom.

This was no more than true. It would have been useless for Caesar to hanker after military commands such as had fallen into the lap of his contemporary, Pompey. Unable for the present to command power in this way, he had turned his attention to control of the popular mob.

The role of the people in the Roman state was important. They elected the magistrates and could pass laws. Since Rome was not policed, the political struggle had been getting for a long time increasingly rowdy. Toughs were frankly for hire, and strong-arm methods were unscrupulously used. Things had not, however, reached a point where people like Caesar appeared openly to organize street fighting. It was rather that elections had to be bought or that in a particular crisis a man with the gangs in his pay could get things done. The qualities needed for power were a capacity for underground intrigue, a bottomless purse, and a power of appealing to the people's sentiment.

Among the people, Caesar's Marian connections were strongly in his favor; and he did not allow them to be forgotten. When his aunt Julia died, he had the death mask of Marius brought out from its niche in the family shrine and carried in her procession with its military honors around it. Such a demonstration, unheard of since Sulla's day, made a great impression. Later, he had the memorials of Marius fresh-gilded and set up overnight in the very places whence Sulla had torn them down. Public opinion might be unsure of the point of these gestures. Were they idle vanity or a bid for power? At all events, the people liked them. Snobs at heart and always accustomed to being officered by aristocrats, they also liked being courted by the dandy of the smart set. No doubt about it, Caesar's influence had ramifications which became very difficult to measure.

None of this would have got him far if he had not been able to lavish a great deal of money on the people. Caesar was not especially rich, and long before he was halfway up the ladder of office, his debts were notorious. He undertook, for instance, the office of aedile, which was always popular with ambitious men because the aedile celebrated the public games. A sum for the purpose was granted from the treasury, but an aedile won favor by expending a great deal

of his own money besides. At the games of Caesar the very
cages of the wild beasts in the procession were of silver,
while the number of gladiators he produced was hitherto
unheard of. Some people have the capacity to float in seas of
debt, and Caesar proved himself such a one. Presently, moreover, he made an ally who could afford what he needed.

An important figure of this time was the millionaire
Crassus, also an aristocrat, yet representing mercantile and
banking interests outside the Senate. Crassus, too, was
forced to look beyond the conservative party. The influence
and political flair of Caesar suited him, while the money
which he controlled was useful to Caesar. Their political ob-
jects were similar enough, being concentrated on rising to
power in despite of the Senate. Their method was to put
forward impecunious aristocrats for office. These people,
unable to pay election expenses themselves, were ready to
promise to introduce various measures their paymasters
wanted.

Such secret bargains would have been more successful if
these instruments had been more respectable ones. Conservatives, however, also possessed much money and bribed
freely. As it was, schemes were hatched in the dark and
checkmated, sometimes unwittingly, leaving behind them a
feeling that Crassus and Caesar were dangerous politicians
whose proceedings ought to be probed — if one knew how
to do it.

Matters had reached this point by 63, when Catiline stood
against Cicero for the consulship. Now Catiline was a
typical instrument of Crassus and Caesar, extravagant,

bankrupt, unscrupulous, yet of sufficient rank to become consul. They were certainly backing him, though Catiline, out for his own ends, was far from easy to control. He talked and threatened too much, so that the conservatives put their enormous influence into the scale, electing Cicero and the cipher, Antonius.

At this point Catiline's interests and those of his pay-masters began to diverge. He had lost the election largely through his own fault. Crassus's money was less likely to be lavished on his cause a second time. When Catiline began to plot an armed revolution, including a canceling of debts, the scheme could not possibly recommend itself to a financier. Why should Crassus support a bankrupt group of gangsters out for plunder? Caesar, who was deep in debt, might have been supposed to like them better. No doubt Caesar was in closer personal contact also, since the details of intrigue were entrusted to him. His influence in the case of an upris-ing might be important.

For reasons such as these, Caesar knew of Catiline's plot. He was far too intelligent to lend himself to such a scheme, but his position was awkward. No doubt he was deeply in-volved with all the principals, and his proceedings had not been intended to bear the light of day. It could have been easy for them to pretend that he had supported the entire conspiracy. Nevertheless, he had to take the risk of exposing it; and he did quietly add his voice to the warnings which Cicero received. Thereafter, he let matters take their course. Everybody suspected that he had a hand in the plot, but nobody proved it. His position was especially awkward during that momentous debate when the Senate empowered Cicero to put the conspirators to death. On that occasion, all eyes were on Caesar when his turn came to give his opinion. If he voted for death, they would think him a coward, since all imagined that he was a secret member of the plot. If, on the other hand, he asked for acquittal, he would convict himself. Caesar's adroitness was equal to the occasion. He pressed for imprisonment wherever and for as long as Cicero pleased. There was no reason to bring the accused to trial as yet. They could be held captive for years if need be until the public sensation had died away. But for his part, Caesar felt that they must be tried before execution.

The moment of danger passed in this way. The conspirators were put to death, and no one accused Caesar. The revolt was suppressed. Cicero's boasting even lent a slightly ridiculous air to a serious crisis. Caesar was actually able to be elected praetor and then departed to a province in Further Spain, still so loaded with debt that Crassus was forced to put up an enormous sum before his creditors would let him leave.

He spent a year in Spain and was highly successful in an unimportant place which attracted small notice. Not only was his administration sound, but he had the opportunity of embarking on a border war. It was his first experience in serious command and his first military service since his twenties. It startled nobody that he was successful. Roman governors were expected to turn their hand to war, and even Cicero proved able to do so. The year, however, must have shown Caesar that he had military talents. It also in passing

restored his financial position, partly from booty, and partly
no doubt from exactions in his province. Since these were a
matter of course, it is merely interesting to note that Caesar
had governed so well that he was not followed back to
Rome by the curses of his outraged subjects.

In general one may say that the year in Spain gave Caesar
confidence. He had been a long while approaching power by
devious means, and now suddenly he was in a hurry. From
the time of the praetorship, there is no stopping his relent-
less advance. He was already forty, and it is said that about
this time he shed tears on being reminded of Alexander the
Great who at his age was dead after conquering the world.
Consuming ambition, so long concealed, now mastered Caesar entirely.

This was evident on his return from Spain, where his ex-
ploits had entitled him to a triumph. This highest honor that
the State could bestow on its military men was coveted by
every noble Roman with absolute passion. Caesar was no
exception to the rule, but he also wanted to stand for the
consulship without delay. This demanded a personal appearance inside the city. If he entered, however, he automatically laid down his command and was not entitled to
the triumph. Accordingly Caesar, encamped at the city
gates, sent a request to the Senate that he might be exempted from coming in to canvass in person. The Senate,
which had no more love for Caesar than it had for Catiline,
refused the favor. Most Romans would have put off their
consulship for a year and held their triumph. Caesar, how-

ever, laid down his command and went inside the city. He was in a hurry for power.

He had learned, no doubt, from the experience of Catiline that the money of Crassus would not buy office in a case where the Senate felt strongly. More support was needed. Caesar looked around and found it in the veteran soldiers of the victorious Pompey.

The famous coalition between Pompey, Caesar, and Crassus which raised Caesar to the consulship was his suggestion. He had something vital to offer to each of his allies, always provided that as magistrate he could get things done. To Pompey and Crassus, this risk was worth taking. Caesar in person was a far better instrument than the worthless characters whom he and Crassus had earlier put forward. But it was one thing to rule the Roman streets and win an election, quite another to put through any program. The second consul, a man named Bibulus, was a conservative and possessed a power of veto over his colleague. Tribunes also, ten of them, had powers of veto. Quite inevitably, a number of these were conservatives.

Caesar's consulship opened briskly. He wasted no time in proposing his measures to the Assembly. The other consul came down in state to interpose his veto. He was shouted at, hustled, and when he still persisted, beaten violently about the head and face and driven from the Forum. The tribunes, attempting to interfere, were similarly treated. Eventually Bibulus, fairly driven off the streets, was forced to take refuge in a curious, antiquarian protest. He shut himself up in his house, where he daily published a notice that he was "watching the skies." Now when a consul watches the skies, he is looking for omens of good luck or bad, which are shown by the flight of birds. But a consul, as head of state, is so important that if he sees a bad omen, public business must at once be interrupted. By an extension of this reasoning, when a consul is formally *looking* for omens, no public business may be transacted. Because, of course, at any moment, he may see one. Thus Bibulus's protest meant that anything which was done during his consulship was illegal.

All this was very clear, but Caesar took no notice. Indeed, it suited him well that Bibulus, shut up in his house all year, should leave the government entirely in Caesar's hands. Illegal actions mattered nothing — for the moment. As a magistrate in office he could not be impeached, while one of the measures which he put through the Assembly gave him Gaul for the next five years as a proconsul. After that, let the conservatives bring him to trial if they could. In five years, much might happen.

The rage of the Senate knew no bounds. Caesar was trampling on every provision of the constitution which was intended to prevent one man from becoming too powerful. He was doing it openly, shamelessly, using strong-arm methods which did not even spare the honored person of his co-head of state. To be sure, his proceedings look a little less outrageous when one studies the political methods of both parties over the previous fifty years. All the same, without a doubt he had descended to new levels, setting precedents which were soon to result in absolute breakdown of the Re-

publican system. In doing so, he showed a contempt for the
constitution which he did not trouble to conceal, either now
or later.

In this atmosphere of political fury, Caesar prepared his
departure for Gaul. It was his intention while there to build
up an army and a military power which could rival Pompey's. Naturally, he did not wish his enemies to gain power
in his absence and pass a law to supersede him. Crassus and
Pompey, influential though they were, had not his skill in
controlling affairs. Besides, Pompey might easily become de-
tached if he grew jealous. All in all, Caesar felt anxious. He
cemented the alliance by giving Pompey in marriage the
hand of his daughter Julia. Her mother, Cornelia, had been
some time dead; and Caesar had at one time been married
to Pompeia, a cousin of Pompey's. He had divorced her,
however, and now allied himself with Calpurnia, daughter
of Piso, a supporter in the Senate whose election as consul
he procured for next year. Having thus protected his rear as
well as he could, he tried to win over the most outraged
because the most sincere of his critics, Cicero.

Failing, Caesar set Clodius on to drive Cicero into exile.
The position of Clodius vis-à-vis Caesar is now worth detail-
ing because it illustrates as clearly as anything can how completely unscrupulous Caesar as a politician was. Clodius, a
youngish, dissolute man, appears to have been having an intrigue with Pompeia, Caesar's wife. Considering Caesar's
own reputation, he was perhaps not in a position to blame
her. At all events, he made no move in the matter until
Clodius precipitated a scandal.

The secret rites of the Good Goddess, for women only, were yearly performed in the house of one of the ladies of aristocratic Rome. Pompeia was selected in 62 and presided under the instruction of her mother-in-law Aurelia, who had been priestess earlier. Out of mere reckless mischief Clodius, who dressed up well as a girl, determined to be present and persuaded Pompeia to agree. He was duly admitted in disguise by Pompeia's servant; but he happened to come at a crucial moment in the rites, and the girl could not stay with him. Left to himself for a while, he was presently discovered by a maid of Aurelia's who recognized him for a man. Immediately she went to her mistress. Aurelia, breaking off the rites, instituted a search, and Clodius was caught.

This matter should have ended with the trial of Clodius for sacrilege and the divorce of Pompeia by her husband. Clodius, however, had qualities of a sort which made him a desirable henchman of Crassus and Caesar. Crassus therefore bought the jury off by bribes notorious even in that corrupt age, while Caesar airily refused to bear witness against him. He did divorce his wife, though he said he had nothing but other people's suspicions to go on. "The wife of Caesar," he remarked when tackled on the subject, "should be above suspicion."

This Clodius was now employed to compass the exile of Cicero. His methods were Caesar's own with an exaggeration of the precedent Caesar had set. Master of Crassus's power and Pompey's power, Clodius led the street gangs in person, posting them as though for a military operation and driving opponents from the Forum in pitched battles. Nothing could be done for a couple of years until the conservatives hired gladiators and in open combat killed him. It is hardly surprising that a few years later still, the street fighting in Rome reached such a pitch that the Senate named Pompey sole consul and had him bring in troops to restore order.

Caesar's conquests in Gaul now opened the eyes of the Romans to the real nature of his greatness. Accustomed though people then were to amateur soldiers, they were astounded that this politician, this dandy, this epileptic should be one of the great masters of war. Caesar proved his abilities in countries which were uncivilized, often trackless. In his day the commander in chief marched with his armies, sharing inevitably in their exertions. Nor was this all. From the very first moment when he left Rome at a gallop for Gaul, Caesar's movements left his contemporaries gasping. It was not merely that he had the faculty of quick decision, the instinct which tells a man when a daring advance will pay better than waiting for supports. It was also that his own methods of getting about were headlong. Escorts and horses were left floundering behind him. Caesar, accompanied often by secretaries to whom he dictated from horseback, could ride like one possessed.

Even when the legions went to winter quarters, Caesar himself had three provinces to govern: that of Gaul, which was the south of France; that of Cisalpine Gaul, which was North Italy; and that of Illyria, or the Dalmatian coast. He spent his winters on the Italian side of the Alps, holding assizes and dealing with problems. Illyria, for instance, was wild country and had recently been conquered. Until Caesar required the legions in Gaul, two had been stationed at Ravenna convenient to the Illyrian border. It was now necessary to control this province without them.

Such tasks needed brilliant qualities, and Caesar had them. He was not, however, a soldier of mere dash and daring. Few commanders have been better engineers. When it came to bridging the swift Rhine or using fortifications or fighting a naval war in Atlantic conditions against a seafaring people, Caesar always had the intellectual resources needed. He had moreover something else which explains his mastery over the imaginations of his soldiers. It is strange that Caesar, so clearsighted and cool over practical problems, should be in some ways a romantic; but he was so. He really had a sense of the greatness and glamor of conquest. This lifted him over the terrible business of war, the greed for plunder, and the hunger for power in Rome. When he sailed to conquer Britain, he was going to the edge of the known world across an ocean whose tides and storms were vast and uncontrolled. He had with him eight hundred ships, out of which a hundred and fifty were built by private persons at their own cost. It was known that Britain was a poor country, that plunder would not be extraordinarily great. It was not greed that built these ships, but rather that Caesar had a sense of adventure which he had managed to communicate to those who were going with him.

He was no mere visionary, however, any more than he was a mere politician. When he turned a limited war for defense of the Roman province into the conquest of Gaul, he did not do so entirely for love of adventure or for ambition. It was obvious to his clear eye that Gaul, divided among warring tribes, must fall prey either to Germans or to Rome. The invading Germans, far more aggressive and savage than the Gauls, were dangerous neighbors. Their natural frontier was the Rhine, whence it would be easier for Rome to control them. Nor were the interests of the Gauls themselves to be advanced by letting them be conquered by savage tribes. Rome had more to offer than the Germans. Amid all the horrors which war undoubtedly brought on Gaul, Caesar consistently displayed an interest in the country's future. He made, for instance, friends among Gauls. In early youth, his tutor had been a learned Gaul from North Italy. Caesar had always espoused the cause of these people, who were excluded from the privileges granted to other Italians. He now broadened his interests to include the Gauls beyond the Alps, not only from the Roman province, but even from among the chiefs of the Long-haired Gauls, in other words, those independent of the Romans.

War is a terrible business, perhaps no more brutal in those days than it is now. Yet Caesar was cruel in different ways from our modern ones, displaying that cool-blooded quality which his biographers noted. Comparatively speaking, it was simple to conquer Gaul at first. The tribes were divided, so that those who held out could be subdued with the aid of the others. Yet liberty is a precious thing. It soon became apparent to all the tribes at once that their new master was going to have matters his way. They did not like it; and suddenly all of Gaul was in rebellion. Once more in a brilliant campaign, Caesar conquered; but the embers of revolt would not be stamped out. While resistance still smouldered, there was a chance that Caesar's work would be undone, particularly as events at Rome called him away. It was hardly even to the interests of Gaul that war should drag on. Caesar now determined on a lesson which would not be forgotten. When the citadel of Uxellodunum yielded at last, containing desperadoes who had taken refuge there from all over Gaul, Caesar deliberately spared their lives but cut off their hands. This terrible action in effect concluded the Gallic War. In the Civil War which followed, though Caesar's legions took part, the Gauls lay quiet. In the next generation, the flowering of civilization in Gaul justified Caesar's conquest.

He probably had always intended to write a history of the war. It was a literary age, and many of his officers wrote their own accounts or composed their epic poems with the Gallic War as a theme. Time hung heavily on the hands of an active young man in winter quarters. Caesar, however, spent hardly any time in winter quarters. The winter season was no time of rest for him. He had his North Italian province and Illyricum to administer. He must go there in person, hold the assizes, consult with his deputies. He must busy himself with the questions of remounts, supply, and recruiting. Written in the intervals of constant travel and bustle by a man who was conducting a major war in person, *The Gallic War* is an extraordinary tribute to Caesar's capacity for getting things done. It bears no marks of haste. The easy polish of its lucid style is never marred by rough spots which he has left unfinished. The simplicity of its narrative conceals the expert propagandist. Naturally Caesar is concerned to set forth his own view of the war, but he is too intelligent to distort the facts. Instead, he marshalls them and lets them speak for themselves. The reputation of *The Gallic War* does not depend entirely on its firsthand authority. It has qualities of style and intellectual power which mark Caesar as a writer of the first rank. His achievement, considerable for any man, becomes remarkable in one of such constant movement, furious action, and dubious health.

Caesar had gone to Gaul to create himself an army rivaling Pompey's. He had five years for the task, but it was not enough. Nearing the end of his term, he sought an extension. Pompey and Crassus came up to meet him at Luca, a little town of no importance which was just inside his North Italian province. Here the next five years were mapped out by the three principals who now in effect governed Rome. Shamelessly also, while the Republic in name still existed, respected Senators, financiers, ambitious young men came up to Luca. All had interests of their own to advance and did not scruple to court the men in power, even when they disliked them.

The day of clever politics was over, and military force alone would count in the future. All three perceived this, and decided upon measures which recognized this fact. Crassus must have an army if he were to remain at the top. He received one and license to use it in a war with the Parthian Empire on the Euphrates. He set out east to be defeated and killed and to vanish from history. His disappearance left two great rivals in the state, and thereby increased the chance of civil war between them.

Pompey required to keep up an army rivaling Caesar's. He was granted the provinces of Spain and the unconstitutional permission to govern them from Rome, sending out to Spain his lieutenants and being allowed to raise troops. This had the further advantage that when Crassus perished, Pompey was on hand to be entrusted with a campaign to avenge him. He was therefore able to collect still more legions both in Italy and the East, while delaying departure. In this fashion, Pompey grew great in Rome. The affairs of the Republic had reached such a point that without his soldiers, it could not be governed at all.

Caesar for his part had received an extension of his Gallic command until March 49. Since the new year began in January, proconsuls could not be appointed to succeed him during that year. It was his intention to be consul himself in 48, and with no nonsense about a personal canvass. By stepping instantly from his Gallic command into consulship, he would be out of reach of the Senate, which still wanted to bring him to trial for his illegal acts before going to Gaul. Once the conservatives had him a private citizen in Rome, which Pompey's army controlled, he would be at their mercy.

Caesar understood perfectly well that his life depended on keeping his command till the end of the year. If the Senate, by passing some extraordinary measure, could find a substitute for him in March, 49, he could only defend himself by war. This was a solution neither he nor Pompey desired, both possibly uncertain of the outcome. Their alliance, however, had been ruptured by the death of Julia in child-birth. The rise of Caesar as a soldier was naturally unwel-come to the man who had been Rome's general for a genera-tion. Pompey, conservative, hesitant, no real politician, was influenced by what his senatorial friends urged upon him. Worse still, he did not restrain them from extreme measures. A proposal to supersede Caesar came up and was vetoed by tribunes in Caesar's pay. The Senate, casting caution to the winds, proclaimed martial law, entrusting Pompey with the government. The tribunes, one of whom was Mark Antony, fled in fear of their lives. Caesar, waiting on the borders of his North Italian province, perceived his enemies had played into his hands. Had they not driven the elected magistrates of the people to take refuge with him? Immediately, he gave secret orders to his troops which set them on the move, while he in person displayed himself at a public festival as though there was nothing on his mind. During dinner, he excused himself for a brief while, got into a carriage which was waiting, and set out after his men. The war had started.

Caesar's forces were handy in Gaul, and they were battle-trained. Pompey's were scattered in Italy, Spain, and the East. It was easy for Caesar to maneuver his rival out of Italy, but the resources of Pompey were great. He retired to Greece, accompanied by most of the leaders of the State, even including many who had fought in Gaul with Caesar. This was a moment when the future of the world was at stake and private connections mattered little.

The contrast between the two generals now became evi-dent. Pompey, encumbered by much advice from important people, sent his lieutenants to collect soldiers from the East while he waited for gradual increase of power. Caesar after a few weeks in Rome was off to Spain, where he disposed of Pompey's lieutenants there in a lightning campaign. Returning to Italy, which Pompey in his absence had not invaded, he found himself cut off from Greece by Pompey's powerful fleet. It was, however, now getting late in the year so that winter dominated the Mediterranean. Taking advantage of a lack of vigilance due to this fact. Caesar got half his army across, only to find himself cut off from the rest with insufficient forces to face those Pompey had with him.

He nearly paid heavily for his daring. Luckily, Pompey preferred to wait for further reinforcements approaching from the East. Eventually Caesar's forces were reunited in the nick of time; and Pompey, still superior in strength, offered battle.

The fate of Rome was decided at Pharsalus. Pompey, beaten, fled to Egypt with a few companions, where he was murdered. Caesar, following with characteristic dash, found himself involved in a turmoil due to rivalry for the Egyptian throne between Cleopatra and her brother. Caesar and Cleopatra were besieged in Alexandria and only rescued after a three months' siege which allowed his enemies, scattered and broken though they were, to coalesce.

A strange thing happened now. This new world conqueror, with Rome at his feet and everybody waiting to see what he would do, delayed in Egypt. Three months after the siege, he and Cleopatra were still there. Caesar at forty-four years of age was captivated by a princess of twenty-two. Perhaps it was her position which dazzled him. The kings of Egypt were worshiped as divine. There is a suggestion that the glamour of the East had gone to his head. He sailed, it is said, far up the Nile and dreamed of penetrating to the hidden sources of that legendary river. Romantic visions of Alexander chased across his mind. Whether Cleopatra figured in these dreams or not seems uncertain. At all events, she bore him a son whom she named Caesarion.

He tore himself away at last. It was high time. There was a local revolt to crush in Pontus. Two bitter struggles against the Pompeians lay ahead, the first in North Africa, the second once more in Spain. Since the outbreak of war over two years back, Caesar had spent only scattered weeks in Rome. Important people like Cicero were waiting to learn their fates at his hand. The whole machinery of government needed his personal revision.

Two more years raced by amid these preoccupations, and the form of the future began to emerge. Caesar excelled in rapid decisions. He was inexhaustible in sensible plans for organizing the incoherent empire which the Roman Republic had become. He put through a good local government law, admitted North Italian Gauls to the citizenship, reformed the calendar to conform with the sun, repressed corruption, planned roads and cities, a port at the mouth of the Tiber, an isthmus canal at Corinth, the draining of the Pontine marshes. Useful projects of one sort and another poured out of him; and it was noted that architects and planners seemed more important in his mind than the Fathers of the old Republic.

This attitude gave offense, the more so as Caesar did not trouble to conceal it. Toward Republicans he had been very forgiving, lavishing pardons wholesale, even on those like Decimus Brutus who had been his own lieutenant in Gaul before fighting against him. Only men who, once forgiven, rejoined his enemies were condemned to death. Even then Caesar allowed his personal friends and lieutenants to beg off prisoners, well knowing that in civil war a man's dearest relations may be found on the opposite side. As a result, the remaining Senators to a very large extent owed Caesar their lives. Far from being grateful, they darkly suspected that they were quietly marked down for future disfavor.

For these reasons, all hated Caesar. Meanwhile, his contempt for the old forms was plain to everyone who loved the Republic. In Caesar's planning, Rome was capital, not ruler of her empire. Consuls and other magistrates were to be partly local and partly honorary. When a consul died a few hours before the expiration of his year, Caesar held a mock election, solemnly raising a man to the consulate for less than a day. The Senate was reduced to an advisory body. Caesar diluted it with all sorts of excellent people who had previously not qualified to belong. All such measures, even if sensible, were bitterly offensive to old-style patriots. Worse than anything were the personal honors which were heaped upon him.

Caesar was consul. He was dictator. He was censor. He was entitled "Father of his Country." That old legend about the descent of the Julians from Venus was hastily revived. In solemn procession Caesar's image was carried among the gods. His statue was set up in the temple of Quirinus, inscribed "To the invincible God." In fact, it looked probable that Caesar would soon be an official god. This arrangement was not uncommon in the East, where kings were worshiped almost as a matter of course. Even prominent Romans were honored in temples there. In Rome, however, such doings were thought disgraceful. In addition, they suggested that Caesar intended to become king.

Did he desire it? Almost certainly he did. Caesar was dreaming again. His health was giving trouble, and his epileptic fits were more frequent. He was dreaming all the same about Alexander and the conquest of the East as far as India. Where could he not go with his invincible legions? Across the Euphrates lay the Parthian Empire, which had destroyed Crassus. That defeat had never been avenged. Pompey had talked of it, but put the matter off. Now Caesar raised it again and started collecting the troops and the supplies. His supporters pointed out that only by going as king could he have sufficient dignity to impose his rule on the East. The matter culminated in Antony's famous offer of a crown which Caesar put aside. Had the incident been arranged to test the feeling of the people? Republicans thought so.

In the midst of plans of this sort, rumors abounded. Cleopatra had by now come to Rome and was plainly trying to get Caesar into her power. Suppose he put away his wife, who was childless, and married the woman who had already

given him a son? Suppose together they turned their backs
on Rome and centered their empire on one of the cities of
the East, reducing the mistress of the world to the status of
a mere province? Divine honors, grandiose plans, a foreign
woman, contempt of ancient forms fanned personal hatreds
which were already intense. Murder was in the air, and even
Caesar felt it to some degree. Yet he for once was not clear
on his course. Complaining he was hated, he yet dismissed
his bodyguard. The truth of the matter seems to be that he
was courting the popular favor and did not desire to seem
afraid. As he so often had done before, he gambled with
safety. This time at last the dice came up against him.

There are tales of dreams and omens, even stories that
people tried to warn him. There were some sixty people, it
appears, involved in the plot against him, headed by Marcus
Brutus, son of a brilliant woman who had been a prominent
member of Caesar's circle. It was decided to commit the
murder in the Senate House itself because the Senators by
tradition were unarmed. Caesar would have no weapon,
while his opponents would conceal daggers in their togas. A
petition would give them an excuse to crowd around him.
The petitioner in traditional fashion would clasp Caesar's
hands. Then he would hold on tight, while the others struck.

So it was planned, and so it happened. When Caesar felt
the first blow, he cried out and tried to wrench himself free.
But the others were on him, all eager to have their share in
the deed. Unarmed and aging though he was, Caesar strug-
gled for life. The little crowd swayed this way and that as he
fought to get out. It is said that he only gave up at last when

Brutus struck. "You too, Brutus!" he gasped, and, bleeding from many wounds, attempted to draw a fold of his toga over his face. He fell, ironically, at the base of the statue of his old friend and conquered enemy, Pompey. Here Caesar died; but the Republic for the sake of which the murder was done had died already.

AUGUSTUS

Caius Julius Caesar Octavianus, 63 B.C.–A.D. 14

CAESAR'S daughter had died while he was campaigning in
Britain, leaving him without heirs. His sister, however, had
several children. Two nephews served with Caesar in Gaul,
neither of whom showed much promise. Accordingly, when
he became master of Rome, he made the acquaintance of a
great-nephew, Caius Octavius, a boy of fifteen or sixteen
who seemed to show qualities which might make him interesting. Caesar took pains to bring the boy forward, gave
him honorary offices, allotted him a prominent place in his
triumphal procession, and planned to give him experience in
campaigning.

Unfortunately, Octavius was delicate. In presiding over
games as deputy for Caesar, he got sunstroke. Consequently, when Caesar set out for his last battles in Spain,
Octavius was too ill to go with him. His disappointment
pleased Caesar, as did his haste to join his uncle when
he was well enough. By then, however, Caesar in his rapid
way had destroyed his enemies and was bringing tranquillity
to Spain. The incident confirmed his approval of his young
great-nephew. When later in Rome he took the step of

making his will, preliminary to his intended eastern conquest, he named Octavius his heir, formally adopting him as
his son. Proceeding, meanwhile, in his plans for the young
man's education, he sent him to Greece, where commanders
were collecting forces for the eastern campaign. It was his
intention that Octavius should become familiar with the
details of raising and outfitting armies. Since, however, the
boy could not be put in charge of the business, he was
nominally pursuing his education in Apollonia which, like
many of the Greek cities, had a school of rhetoric and philosophy. Thus occupied in the society of a few close friends of
his own, Octavius was rudely startled by the murder of Caesar.

What should he do? He had no official standing in his
great-uncle's world, was hardly grown up. In Rome, the murderers had promptly been hailed as Liberators by the
Senate. It was true that the Senators had confirmed Caesar's
acts, induced to do so by the need to maintain their own
appointments to governorships and other offices. It was true
also that they had conceded to Antony, Caesar's lieutenant,
a public funeral for Caesar. All the same, they had approved
the deed. Some of the officers whom Caesar had in Greece,
beside themselves with sorrow and anger, urged a march on
Rome. The men, they said, would follow Caesar's nephew.

The boy who was faced with this momentous decision was
a short, fair lad, bright-eyed and handsome in a frail way
which made him look even younger than he was. His father,
Octavius, son of an Italian banker, had gone into public life
and risen to be praetor. He had, however, died early. Cae-

sar's niece Atia had then been married to Lucius Philippus, a prominent Senator who had been a good stepfather to Octavius and his sister. The boy had been quietly brought up, less in Rome than in his stepfather's country villas. Intelligent, serious-minded, puritanical, he had little acquaintance with the fashionable set. At the moment, his intimate friend was Marcus Vipsanius Agrippa, whose origins were obscure.

At this time of great shock when older men about him were urging a mad course, Octavius kept his head. Thanking the soldiers, he declined their offer and set out for Italy. Arriving, he was met immediately by his mother and stepfather with even more momentous news. Caesar's will had been published, adopting Octavius and naming him his heir. It was a position which few would envy him. Brutus and Cassius were bound to suspect him as a future avenger; while Antony, who had hoped to be named heir himself, would certainly be jealous. Indeed, Atia and Philippus both implored him to reject the honor for his safety's sake. Antony was by now dominant at Rome. He had impounded Caesar's fortunes and his private papers and was busy getting everything into his hands. Mark Antony was an unscrupulous man entirely lacking in the genius of Caesar. He did, however, have his share of that great force and swiftness which Caesar had possessed and which he demanded of those who served beneath him. In other words, Antony was thoroughly dangerous, no fit opponent for an inexperienced boy with no other backing than a dead man's famous name.

Undeterred by arguments such as these, Octavius proceeded to Rome and made formal application to take Caesar's name in the customary way and to receive his inheritance. Antony, amused and contemptuous, brushed him off, refusing both. Octavius, who had already sent messengers to Greece to get possession of Caesar's campaign funds, paid off the legacies out of his own resources. This bought him immense popularity with the mob and with Caesar's veterans. His insistence on being allowed to take the name of Caesar Octavianus became a nuisance.

Antony tried the effect of a direct quarrel, but Octavius was already too formidable to be pushed aside. Moreover, Antony's troubles at the time were very great. His power extended little beyond Rome. Brutus and Cassius had gone to the East, where they were raising armies. Provincial governors who did not side with them were just as likely to be out for their own ends as to support Antony. In other words, though Antony had established himself for the time as Caesar's successor, he faced contenders more powerful than the boy Octavius. In the meantime, he was already embroiled with Decimus Brutus, who commanded the North Italian province and would not submit to him.

Octavius, meanwhile, had been cultivating the Senate and in especial Cicero. The great orator, optimistic by nature, had high hopes of this inexperienced boy, so deferential and eager to learn. Cicero impressed upon him that love of Republican freedom which was the passion of his own life. Perhaps Octavius would become another Pompey who, having raised himself to high command in the State, would lay it down.

Thus reasoned Cicero, anxious for instruments to use against Antony, in touch with Brutus and Cassius and with Decimus Brutus, also. The state needed an army to deal with Antony, who had Decimus Brutus shut up in Mutina. The consuls, experienced men, could lead it; but the figure of Caesar's legitimate heir would induce the legions to march. Cicero's persuasions were weighty and the times desperate. The name of Caesar Octavian, as the young man was now called after formal adoption, did indeed appeal to Caesar's veterans. Octavian left with the consuls to drive Antony from the siege of Mutina.

The campaign was successful. It soon turned out, however, that Cicero had miscalculated in two important respects. It had not occurred to him that both consuls might be killed in the fighting, leaving Octavian in sole control of the State's army. Nor had he plumbed the boy's mind. The new Caesar had no intention of throwing in his lot with Decimus Brutus, one of the murderers of his father. All he wanted was sufficient power to make Antony see reason. What followed was an alliance between Octavian, Antony, and Lepidus, most important of Caesar's remaining lieutenants. These three now divided power. Together they drew up long lists of those who must die, including Cicero.

What sort of young man was this who, coming from nowhere at the age of eighteen, had made himself the equal of Mark Antony? Without ever serving in armies, he had commanded them. Without ever entering on public life, he had hoodwinked men older than his father. Without apparent qualm, he had signed the death warrants of people who

were famous before he was born. Physically a weakling, he
was hardly even able to bear the stress of campaigning. He
was too ill to take any part in the defeat of Brutus and
Cassius at Philippi.

Yet though Antony had done the work, he was forced to
share the spoils. There was a tough quality about Octavian
which could not be beaten. He was junior partner, of course.
When they divided the world, Antony took the East, arsenal
of great armies, center of Caesar's dreams of conquest. The
East, pacified by the destruction of Brutus and Cassius, commanded resources to make it self-sufficient. The Parthian
war loomed ahead, but the Parthians were an opportunity,
not a drawback. The lost horizons of Alexander's conquests
still attracted the ambitious. Cleopatra, the descendant of
Alexander's successors, had her plans if Antony did not. The
East, potentially, was a source of greatness.

For Octavian, there remained the West. Italy, bankrupt,
no longer self-sufficient, was almost besieged in her own sea.
Sextus Pompey, son of the great Pompey, part exile, part sea
pirate, swelled his forces with runaway slaves or fugitives
from the proscriptions. Already he controlled Sicily, cutting
Rome off from her great granary there, and also from North
Africa, under the dominion of Lepidus and only suspiciously
friendly. Gaul was undeveloped, Spain totally ravaged. The
Roman Senate muttered sullenly as it did what it was told.
Caesar's veterans, meanwhile, demanded farms. The State
being nearly bankrupt, confiscation provided these. The dispossessed in mutinous beggary swelled the ranks of brigands
or fled to Sextus Pompey.

In such a situation Rome accepted her new ruler. He was cautious, incorruptible, hardworking. Unlike the great Julius, he did not dream. Caesar Octavian's feet were on the ground. He was narrow-minded, seeing everything from the Roman point of view, concerned to keep the provinces subordinate, restrict the franchise. As a practical organizer, he was superb; but he proceeded slowly. There was none of that racing genius in him that Julius had. There was none of the impatience, either. He was deferential to the Senate, observed Republican forms, and was careful to hold his power for limited terms, getting regular extensions as the state of emergency was prolonged. The implication always was that he would resign when the crisis was over.

Antony found him difficult to deal with. The truth was, their two natures were quite different. Antony, voluptuous, easygoing, but capable of great effort, was unscrupulous and selfish. He sought power for his private ends, but his methods were casual and open. Octavian, on the other hand, had genuine ideals, partly inherited from Caesar, partly his own. His methods, on the other hand, were secretive. Antony complained of his bad faith. A reconciliation was patched up between them, the forces on both sides being wearied of war. Octavian cemented their alliance by giving Antony the hand of his sister Octavia.

Beautiful, virtuous, intelligent, infinitely kind, endlessly dutiful, Octavia would have made almost anyone a perfect wife. Unfortunately, she bored Antony. His private life was not of this sort, and after living up to her for a while, during the course of which she bore him two daughters, he sent her back to Rome. Thereafter, he went to Egypt and lived with Cleopatra.

Cleopatra in her turn is a personage to whom history has hardly done justice. For there was a touch of greatness about her which was lacking in Antony. Her attraction, which she used quite shamelessly for her own ends, was little to her save a means to her ambition. What she conceived of was something which had been in Caesar's mind at times, an East-West empire in which the East should be predominant. But Cleopatra, too practical to dream of Alexander, was not interested in extending the Empire. She intended, instead, to conquer what there was. Having attempted this through Caesar and having been foiled by his death, she turned deliberately to Antony. She wooed him and won him, providing him with the sort of person and entertainments that he wanted. Antony, a voluptuary and lazy, was at his best when things went wrong. Life was too easy in Egypt. He dallied, mismanaged the Parthian campaign, lost strength and momentum. Meanwhile, hatred for him and Cleopatra grew in Rome.

Octavia was a main cause of this. When Antony sent her home, he did not divorce her, not wishing presumably to make the issue. Octavia consequently lived in his house, brought up his children by an earlier marriage with her own, received his acquaintances, defended his interests, and made herself loved by all. Her injured position bred universal indignation. Two years later, still without divorcing Octavia, Antony married Cleopatra by Macedonian rites which were not legal in Rome. Later still, he sent agents to announce his divorce and turn Octavia out of his house. She, it may be said, not only continued to bring up his older children, but later after his death did the same for those he had by Cleopatra.

For reasons such as these, things drifted toward war; but they did not do so quickly. Problems pressed on Antony and Octavian alike. The world, moreover, was weary of civil war and sought to avoid it. Ten years consequently passed between the battle of Philippi which saw the defeat of Brutus and Cassius and that of Actium. In the meantime, the issues which the two dictators represented were growing clearer.

It was a conflict between East and West. In ten years, Octavian had wrought a transformation in Rome. It had not been easy and had seemed at times slow, but Sextus Pompey was by now driven from the sea, Lepidus from Africa. The raiding of the Alpine and Illyrian tribes which had become a menace was laboriously put down. An amnesty bought exiles back. The confiscation of farms for veterans was at least over. A generation which yearned for peace and security perceived it coming.

A new spirit was in the air. Julius Caesar, in opposition to the ruling caste of his day, had done his work with adventurers like Antony or people like Decimus Brutus, who in a pinch turned against him. By now the aristocracy, decimated, ruined, was positively grateful for help from Octavian in restoring its prestige and fortunes. Meanwhile, the new great men were people of a different background. Marcus Agrippa, immensely able in every practical way, had obscure connections. Gaius Maecenas, a great diplomat, was

Etruscan, not Roman. Such people had an Italian point of view. Long unaccustomed to anything but local independence, they cared little for the cherished freedoms of the Roman state in comparison with order and sound government.

As the old decayed, so the new arose. Octavian had an ideal to offer. He had a great conception of the civilizing influence of Rome, of her history and mission. Rome, however, personified Italy and was but a focus of a destiny Italy shared. Deliberately this national sense, hardly before existing, was built up. The rites of traditional religion were carefully restored. New importations of mysteries from the East were frowned upon. Vergil, a national poet under the patronage of the great Maecenas, was working on the Georgics, elaborate poems on farming and the Italian countryside which were permeated by old folk customs. Agrippa and Octavian himself were beautifying Rome with buildings worthy of the capital of the world.

Set against this, Cleopatra, queen of Egypt, had a different conception to offer, the splendor of divine kingship blazing with eastern riches, remote from its people, yet possessing an overriding authority, a conception of glory welcome to the East. The trouble with it was twofold. In the first place, Antony, her instrument was not quite equal to his role. His organization of the East, often sound, was spoiled by a carelessness which ruined everything. He alternated active and lazy periods, while Cleopatra to preserve her influence with him pandered to this weakness. Yet even this might not have destroyed them, had it not happened that the power on which they depended was Roman. Antony's legions, even when raised in the East, were Roman-officered and Roman in outlook. Roman hatred of Cleopatra and things eastern swelled with the regeneration of Italy, with the sharpening contrast between Octavian and Antony, with that between the blameless Octavia and her Egyptian rival. In the final battle between the two sides at Actium in 31 B.C., Antony's legions deserted. He and Cleopatra committed suicide. Coincidentally, it fell to the lot of the consul of that year to announce to the Romans Antony's defeat and death. The name of that consul was Marcus Tullius Cicero, son and only survivor of the great man whom Antony had caused to be murdered.

At the battle of Actium, Octavian was thirty-two. He had vanquished all rivals and now was master of the world. It remained to him to give some permanent form to his rule which would be able to conciliate Roman feeling, while yet preserving the centralization of power which the Empire needed. He did it by restoring the Republic.

It was only in form, of course. Even the Senators cried out in dismay when asked to take on his problems. As the matter was settled, the border provinces and those where trouble was expected remained under his direct control. He administered them, as Pompey had once done, from Rome, appointing deputies as he saw fit. No precedent was thus broken, while easier provinces were handed back to the Senate. Octavian, however, really controlled these also. Though he restored the consulship to its old dignity, he reserved the right to go through the list of those up for election and to indicate his own choice. He himself was content with the simple title of Princeps, or First Citizen, which had loosely been used of great people during the Republic. He also quietly possessed himself of tribunician power, which made his person sacrosanct, gave him the authority to summon the assembly and propose laws, and allowed him the right of veto. In fact, the Republic went through its stately parade as of old, but nothing happened without the consent of the First Citizen.

In this way the Principate came into being. Without abandoning power, Octavian quietly renounced parade of it. All the same, his peculiar position needed some justification. He found it in an ingenious combination of the ideas of East and West. Worship of the divine ruler was an eastern idea. It had nothing to do with what we think of as religion, but was merely an acceptable way of expressing the difference between a great king and his subjects. To republican Rome, this notion was alien. All the same, the genius, or spirit of the family was universally honored in Rome among the household gods. Abstract figures like Concord or Fortune also had their shrines. Thus both in East and West there existed a distinction between gods who presided over the universe and other conceptions to which it was legitimate to build shrines. In a sense, then, even Rome was ready to make a god of a dead individual whose spirit, or genius, had been outstanding. Accordingly, in the year 40 B.C., Julius Caesar was proclaimed divine. This meant nothing save that the State had no more ultimate compliment to bestow. Such terms, however, are confusing. Octavian now alone among Romans was officially son of a god.

His nature was superhuman besides. Had he not risen among older people who had everything in their favor? Was he not at thirty-two master of the world? It was entirely natural for the East to put up temples to him, and only the cautious nature of the man held back. Godhead, however, would be useful if he could fit it in with Roman tradition. Presently he adopted a new name, Augustus, which means "revered," almost "superhuman." It had been associated with Romulus, founder of Rome. Supremely skillfully, Octavian had combined an idea with which the East was familiar with one traditional at Rome. Equally skillfully, he was never precise about his claims, allowing temples to be put up to the "Genius of Rome and Augustus," never claiming that he was divine himself, but indicating that when he was dead, he might as it were attain to sainthood.

With these cautious claims was combined a modest bearing and a total absence of parade. In the course of his struggle with Sextus Pompey, he had married Pompey's relative, Scribonia, to mark a brief accord. He had not liked Scribonia, however; and the treaty with Pompey did not endure. Marking his disapproval of both in the most offensive way, he divorced Scribonia on the very day that she bore him a daughter, Julia. Shortly after, he really fell in love with Livia, wife of Tiberius Claudius Nero, a nineteen-year-old beauty who had already one son and was about to bear another. Her marriage appears to have been the usual Roman business affair. Nero was perfectly ready to divorce her, merely waiting until her son was born. Octavian then mar-

ried her forthwith, creating a slight scandal even in liberal
Rome. The marriage, however, was ideally happy, save that
there were no children. Livia and Augustus were a model
husband and wife, domestic, devoted, living examples of
what a Roman marriage ought to be. For all his apparent
modesty, Augustus understood that the eyes of the world
were always on him.

The regeneration of Rome was his great task, and he ad-
dressed himself to it with vigor. There were plenty of good
men left. Fine traditions lingered, even more strongly in the
Italian countryside than they did in Rome. They had been
diluted, however, by the influence of slaves from all over the
world who, being very commonly set free after a time, settled down as citizens. Augustus was at pains to limit this
process, especially in the case of slaves of proved bad character. Deliberately also, he set himself to raise the Roman
birthrate.

Families had been growing smaller, partly as a result of
the civil wars, partly because Italian poor were ruined by
the competition of slave labor, and partly because display
among the rich raised the cost of living for aspiring, middle-
class families. Against all these tendencies Augustus set his
face, by his own example, by laws restraining extravagance,
by laws penalizing bachelors and couples with few children.

Even an emperor may find it difficult to oppose economic
trends. The easy money was to some extent still there. The
foreign slaves crowded the households of even moderate families. What could be done by law or example, Augustus did.
Even more important, perhaps, he gave the leading classes

in the State enough to do. Undoubtedly part of the trouble
during the Republic had been the idleness of many wealthy
people. Between magistracies, the Senators had not worked
hard. The Knights, or financiers, had often made money
faster than they knew what to do with it. Excluded,
however, from public life, they did not divert it to public
ends or use their energies for anything but vulgar display. It
happened, however, that there were enormous numbers of
things which were not being done. No public body existed
to supervise the Roman water supply, maintain the banks of
the Tiber against sudden floods, look after public buildings,
repair or plan new Italian roads. All these needed trained
workmen and secretaries, headed by supervisory boards, the
whole apparatus of a civil service. Tax collecting needed
taking out of private hands, which meant establishing a
corps of financial experts. In other words, the whole machinery of state needed overhauling. In the course of it, Augustus had responsible jobs for men of every grade. The
consulship might become a ceremonial office, but it retained
importance as an avenue to administrative positions. In fact,
so great was the demand for people of consular rank, that
presently the term of the office was cut down in order to
obtain them. The Knights, meanwhile, fitted also into the
scheme, particularly in the regions of finance. So successful
was this reorganization that it actually did resign the aristocrats to loss of power. A surprising number of the people
Augustus employed in responsible ways had been prominent
on the other side in the civil wars. The bitterness which is
the usual legacy of such times disappeared as though by

magic. The golden age of Rome rose literally out of ruins which one might have supposed impossible to build on.

The provinces were not neglected either. One thinks of Augustus as administering from Rome. The fact of the matter is, however, that on several occasions he spent years abroad, partly campaigning, and partly settling the affairs of his vast empire. He did this even though his health was not strong. Since his sunstroke, he never went out without a hat; while he wore several thicknesses of tunic and a chest protector under that. In spite of these precautions, he fell ill a number of times, nearly always when he was exposed to the rigors of travel. Notwithstanding, he persevered indefatigably; and where he did not go himself, his minister Agrippa showed equal ability

We think of the age of Augustus as an age of peace, and so essentially it was. Reorganization brought the provinces the good government which hitherto had been theirs only in theory. Suppression of pirates, state encouragement of docks, of maps, of roads and harbors opened up the world. The East in particular hummed with trade and seemed to burst with its own wealth.

Strangely enough, however, when we look more closely, we perceive that this peace is only one side of the story. There was a great deal of war. The Roman Empire, expanded haphazard, this way and that as occasions occurred, had irregular boundaries, illogical, impossible of defence. Even Italy until Octavian's day was raided by the wild tribes in the Alps. Until the frontiers were in some sense regularized, there was no protecting them. It was the task of

Augustus to set them solidly on the Rhine, the Danube, and the Euphrates. For this campaigns were needed all along the northern border. Parts of Spain still had to be subdued. Some sort of agreement was made with the Parthians. The southern frontier of Egypt needed attention, as did the bounds of the North African Province. In other words, continuous expansion went on throughout the reign, and yet it did so without really troubling the profound peace of the civilized parts of the Empire.

The chief reason for this was that Augustus had now in his hands a completely professional army. The pay of the soldiers, their terms of enlistment were standardized. A special treasury was set up, financed by special taxes, to give them their discharge bonus. It was not necessary to flood Italy with returned veterans after each major campaign or to hold levies and recruiting drives for each new undertaking. To be sure, the legions needed replenishing, but the wider diffusion of the Roman citizenship was making it easier to get volunteers. Besides, the development of auxiliary cohorts, some specially armed, some not, went on apace. These people became citizens only on discharge and could be recruited from the warlike tribes lately conquered, many of whom preferred the service to settling tamely down to peaceful existence.

Thus prudently for most of his days Augustus managed to have the best of war and peace. Yet the balance between them was a delicate one to maintain. Toward the end of his reign, partly to gratify the military ambition of young princes of his house, and partly for a convenience which any map will show, he attempted to advance the German frontier from the Rhine up to the Elbe. A number of highly advertised campaigns did not, however, enable the army to winter in those regions. They amounted, in fact, to large-scale raids which had the effect of uniting the warlike German tribes under a great leader. This chief, Arminius, had served for a while with the legions and knew how to handle them. Ambushing the Romans in the midst of difficult country, he wiped out three legions and their commander, Quintilius Varus.

It was the greatest shock of Augustus's life. He was nearly seventy and unable to bear it. Indeed, his anguished cry rings down the ages, "Varus, Varus, give me back my legions!" Yet, curiously, it was at least partly his fault and points up a very grave weakness in the imperial system. Varus had not been the man for the job, but he was connected by marriage with Augustus's house. Thus early in imperial history, it is risky to entrust the legions to the best man. They must be given to those whose loyalty is quite secure and those whose prestige is in some sense the emperor's own.

An even more fatal flaw emerged. The lost legions were not replaced. It would, no doubt have been considered unlucky to give new troops these vanished names. But no new troops were raised. The number of the legions was permanently three less. Could it possibly be that the ingenious balance between war and peace was breaking down? By habituating the civilized world to peace, was Augustus cutting off the recruits that he needed? Time would show.

There were many warlike peoples to defend the Empire still. But time would show.

The great emperor was seventy-six when he died, having risen to power before he was twenty. For over fifty years he had guided Rome, for over forty in sole control of affairs. In summing up his great program of building in the city of Rome itself, he said, "I found Rome brick; I left it marble." The verdict is true in a spiritual sense as well. What we think of as great in Rome was expressed more fully in the Augustan age than in any other. In literature it is dominated by the conception, not merely of Rome's greatness, but of Rome's mission. The *Aeneid* of Vergil, the histories of Livy, the *Odes* of Horace all say the same thing. It is Augustus who imposed this idea on his age, and the success of it is a measure of his greatness. Yet in a personal way it almost swallowed him up. Looking behind it for the man himself, we find him curiously difficult to know. Always conscious that he has a mission, he is eternally controlling his own behavior to suit. To set an example, he wears homespun garments and his wife spins every day. He weighs his lightest words with care, listens patiently and long. He gives time to the performance of antiquarian ceremonies, once religious but now little more than a link with history. He is polite and likes to be approached politely, yet without an undue deference. All this is part of his mask.

Certain things, however, one may see. He was fond of children. In his household there was a regular palace school, through which passed Antony's children, his own stepsons, his grandsons, the children of Herod, and other noble boys.

Among the girls, his daughter Julia, her daughters, and Octavia's also were familiar there. He liked children about him and did not visit their parents' crimes upon them, as some Romans did.

He liked gambling, too. Officially this was one of the things he sought to discourage, but it was one of his rare recreations. He would pass an evening with his family or his friends playing gambling games, sometimes staking people to a sum of money at the start of play, or on other occasions careful not to win more than he should.

He was devoted to his friends as they to him, and his private correspondence would have been a burden even to a man who had no public business. It was very friendly and open. He prays the poet Horace, a man of low-class origin, to treat his house as his own at any time, and to order what he likes. One sees from surviving examples of his writing that Augustus is witty, is cultured, and is master of a plain style which can rise to dignity.

His relations with his wife, his sister Octavia, and his friends indicate inner warmth. With the rest of his family, he was not always fortunate. His delicate position as citizen-emperor was particularly difficult to hand down to an heir. Yet without one, the keystone would be gone and the arch collapse. An heir there must be.

He fixed at first on Marcellus, a beloved and promising son of his sister by a marriage previous to that with Antony. At the earliest moment, Marcellus was married to his own daughter Julia. Shortly thereafter, however, Marcellus died.

Destitute now of heirs, Augustus married his daughter to

his own great friend Agrippa. It was the custom to treat
women as chattels in this way, to marry them for political
reasons to men their fathers' age. Julius Caesar had married
his Julia to Pompey, and the marriage had been happy.
There can be no suggestion that this new Julia was or
thought she was treated unfairly. All the same, one cannot
help feeling sorry for her. Attractive, gifted, rather strictly
brought up and yet flattered by every fashionable group in
Rome, it was hard for Julia to keep her head. She made,
however, a good wife to Agrippa. No sooner were her two
sons in their teens than Augustus began to bring them forward, this time at the expense of Agrippa, who had hitherto
been the apparent heir. Now it seemed he was only to be
guardian to his children. The arrangement, though not completely congenial to Agrippa, might have worked. He, however, died.

Augustus looked around again. The boys were still young
and his own health precarious. There remained his stepsons.
Drusus, the younger, whom he had really liked, was dead.
Tiberius, whom he had never warmed to, would have to do.
Let him marry Julia and act as guardian to his future step-
sons.

There was something cold-blooded about this arrangement which reminds one of young Octavian sitting down
with Antony to draw up that long death-list. Poor Tiberius
was happily married and had a son of his own, whose interests he was now asked to overlook in favor of Julia's children. Julia, who had borne another son, Agrippa Posthumus,
after her husband's death, was once more given in marriage

to a person for whom she had little affection. The result was unhappy. Tiberius withdrew into exile in Rhodes, while Julia, kicking up her heels at last, created such scandals that all Rome shortly knew of them except Augustus.

Augustus did not move in fashionable circles, and it took him a while to discover about his daughter's behavior. When he did so, his rage was even greater than his anguish. All the cold side of his nature felt outrage that his daughter should have made the whole purpose of his life, as it were, ridiculous. He and Livia had been so careful to set a proper example, while behind their backs the whole town sniggered. Refusing so much as to set eyes on Julia or hear her name again, he banished her to a dreary little island off the coast in strict confinement.

Even so, his plans went awry, for his two grandsons died. There was now no one left to succeed but Agrippa Posthumus, only a little boy. Augustus was too old to wait. Besides, the child was abnormal. Something sinister had appeared in the inheritance of the Julian family which was to recur. Nothing could ever be made out of the boy Agrippa.

There was no one left to turn to except Tiberius, middle-aged, unloved, embittered, no blood relation. Even now, Augustus did not give up hope of having descendants. Pushing aside his own son, Tiberius was forced to adopt his nephew, who was married to one of Julia's daughters. The arrangement, unnatural at best, would breed great troubles for the imperial house. Perhaps Augustus had been moving other people about like counters for too long. That will of his had never accepted frustration, and he did not intend Tiberius to stand in the way of his own descendants.

Thus, then, after solving almost every problem but those of his own house, Augustus died. Later generations looked back on his time as a golden age. By doing so, however, they confessed that in his work lay seeds of weakness. Things were not, at least under his descendants, as good again. This is, however, but another way of saying that he was a great ruler, one of the greatest. His achievement was in fact the Roman world. It was the union of all the Mediterranean lands in one civilized whole which has left its traces on history down to this day. This is perhaps a limited achievement compared to that of Plato or of Buddha. It stands, however, on its own feet and does not fear comparisons. It has its value.

VERGIL *and* HORACE

Publius Virgilius Maro, 70–19 B.C.
Quintus Horatius Flaccus, 65–8 B.C.

VERGIL was a North Italian, born near Mantua in what was then the Roman province of Cisalpine Gaul. Gauls had over-run the Po valley more than three hundred years before, but it is not probable that Vergil was Gallic by descent. Many Italians had been drawn thither by the fertility of the region; and Vergil's father seems to have been such a one, a Roman citizen and a man neither well-to-do nor poor. Some say he started out life in the employment of a man named Magius, whose daughter he married. It is certain he soon acquired a farm and that he kept bees. He is also said to have been a potter. Italian pottery, in the beginning at least, was turned out by farmers in their spare time, utilizing the clay of their own fields. By Vergil's day the potter owned slaves, operating with them what amounted to a small factory. The connection, however, between agriculture and pottery had not died. It was still probable that a farmer with surplus money to invest might develop such a factory on his land. This may have been so in Vergil's father's case and would explain why

Vergil, a student for many years, never needed to earn. In any event, the household was simple. None of the luxury of rich Italian villas came Vergil's way in early life.

Either Vergil's father was a more learned man than one might expect, or the boy's talents were early noticed. Vergil had two brothers, both of whom died fairly young. He had also a stepbrother who survived him. It may have seemed as though the dreamy member of the family would respond to education while a brother succeeded to the farm. At all events, when local resources for schooling were exhausted, Vergil was sent to Cremona for what we should now consider a high-school education.

Cremona was a flourishing Cisalpine town, part Gallic, part Roman. Caesar, who was at this moment governor of the province, was in the flood tide of his victories in Gaul. Out of the province tramped young recruits, eager for adventure and glory. Back into it flowed the captured plunder of Gaul. It was a thrilling, hopeful time for the Cisalpines; and its excitement was felt in towns like Cremona, which was a center for recruitment and for the purchase of supplies. It was also an assize town, a place to which Caesar in person came regularly during the winters, dispensing justice.

What did the Cisalpines care about Republican freedom? As subject peoples, they had no share in it. Caesar was the champion of their liberties. Caesar maintained they were ready for self-government and full citizenship like the rest of Italy. Vergil's admiration for Caesar and his successor Augustus is lifelong. He does not mourn the Republic, since he finds in the Empire a larger liberty. He is the Empire's poet.

Higher schooling in Vergil's day was chiefly directed toward forming literary style in Greek and Latin. Much time was spent on figures of speech and devices for embroidering a theme without ever quite losing track of it. Boys learned lists of quotations and mechanical rules. To some extent this was enlarging to the mind, but it was dull. We have a few verses supposed to have been written by Vergil saying, in effect, farewell to school. With more justice than many students, he was glad to be rid of it.

A career at the bar was about the only practical thing which such education led up to. It is a measure of Vergil's ambition or his father's that he soon went on to Rome and studied under a rhetorician fashionable there. It was wasted effort. Tall, ungainly, invincibly shy, with a provincial accent, he had no aptitude for the law-courts. Once more the training was monotonous. In Cicero's day, an aspiring young man had apprenticed himself to some well-known lawyer. By now professional schools had taken over. These posed imaginary problems for debate which were then ornamented by all the tired flourishes of rhetoric. It was like Cremona over again, and the good Vergil gained from it was largely incidental. He made the acquaintance of the big city, which he never loved; and he may have got to know the young Octavian.

Octavian at this time was twelve years old. His grandmother had died; and it fell to his lot to pronounce the public oration which was customary at the funerals of important people. Needing professional coaching, he went to a school of rhetoric. Whether he really, precocious though he was, had much in common with a gangling country boy of seventeen seems doubtful. Possibly Vergil's admiration for Caesar made a connection between them. At all events, we possess a minor poem dedicated to the young Octavian and probably written by Vergil.

A fair number of poems unpublished in Vergil's lifetime are attributed to these early years, and scholars have argued long as to whether he wrote them. On the one hand, they show little sign of future genius and may have been, as it were, attracted by his later reputation. On the other, Vergil was a slow developer. His education taught him to write tolerable verse, but it was only gradually that his capabilities grew. The matter is chiefly important because a number of details connected with Vergil's early life may be deduced from these poems if they are truly his.

For these reasons, there is a good deal of uncertainty about what Vergil did. Tradition says he argued one case in court, which was a failure, and then gave up the bar. He was twenty-one when the civil war between Caesar and Pompey broke out. Some have it that he enlisted in Caesar's army, possibly even served in an early campaign before being discharged on account of ill-health. Most deny this. Certainly he took no major part in the war and was known to be delicate all through his adult life. Diagnosis is impossible, but some of his symptoms suggest that he may have had tuberculosis.

Our feet are on firmer ground when we come to the influences molding his mind. The age of Cicero was a great literary age, at least as interesting as that of Augustus. In particular, in the year 54 B.C. a remarkable poem was published called "On the Nature of Things" by Titus Lucretius.

"On the Nature of Things" is a poem on a grand scale describing the views of the Greek philosopher Epicurus. To Epicureans, the universe is made of atoms moving in empty space and by their combinations creating everything. What dies, decays, is broken up, ceases to exist. Even the soul is made of atoms, as are the gods themselves, untroubled beings who live in a world of their own, caring nothing for men. Thus fears, superstitions, terror of death are a waste of time. There is no afterlife. No prayer, no incantation has any effect. The task of the wise is to live in harmony with the universe around him. When a man does so, he experiences the sensation of pleasure, which is less physical pleasure than spiritual serenity. This state is the highest good. In sum, Epicurus and his disciple Lucretius are scientists, preaching freedom from the irrational fears of their times. Theirs is a lofty conception, if in some respects a negative one. Lucretius has written one of the world's great poems, magnificent in its courage, and glorious in its feeling for nature.

The effect of Lucretius on Vergil was tremendous. In the first place, Lucretius writes in hexameters, the verse form of Homer, which had hitherto been only imperfectly adapted to Latin. This is the verse form which Vergil was to make his own. His artistry, more subtle than that of Lucretius, is only possible because of the earlier poet's work.

In the second place, the gospel preached by Lucretius made a great appeal to Vergil's mind. As a countryman himself, he liked the approach of people who started out with the proposition that things around us are real, not, so to speak, ideas in the mind. He liked the interest of the Epicureans in the processes of nature and their scientific methods of analysis. Educated Romans, dissatisfied with their religion, were looking to Greek philosophy for answers to their needs. As the old Republic broke up, the old standards crumbled. All were groping, Vergil among them. Ultimately he left Rome altogether and settled in Naples, where Siro, a well-known Epicurean, held a school.

In the school of Siro, Vergil passed quiet years while Caesar conquered the world and died, while Antony and Octavian rose to power. Retiring, unworldly, unmarried, he still had connections with a number of able young men who were rising to prominence. There were several reasons for this. The doctrines of Epicurus were fashionable then, while Naples was a resort town for the Roman rich. Vergil's absorbing interest in things of the mind was a refreshment to those who shared his tastes but had less time for them. Besides, Vergil, for all his shy ways, had qualities which made him loved — a gentle sense of humor, a power of penetrating below the surface of things. Nor did he swallow the Epicurean doctrines whole. There was no room in these for the enthusiasm with which Octavian's friends set out to regenerate Rome. Yet though Vergil was not a practical man, his feelings were deep.

In 41, he had need of friends. Octavian, facing the usual demobilization problems after the defeat of Brutus and Cassius, had found a bankrupt treasury incapable of buying farms on which to settle his veterans. Whole districts in

Cisalpine Gaul were therefore seized. Vergil's father, blind or nearly so by now, was dispossessed. Vergil was roughly attacked by the soldier who took over and forced to save his life by swimming a river. Luckily the important people he knew took up his cause. The farm was restored, though the misery of the countryside as a whole remained in his mind.

It was not until those early years of Octavian that Vergil, now in his thirties, published his first poems. The *Eclogues,* songs sung by imaginary shepherds, are in form an imitation of a well-worn Greek model. In fact, however, they are thoroughly Italian. The shepherds are placed in the countryside Vergil knew and are singing not merely of the farmer's life and rural superstitions, but of important events that were going on. The seizure of the Mantuan farm is told, the escape from the soldier, the misery of the dispossessed. Vergil's friends are there, as are the troubles of the past and hopes for the future. In fact, the *Eclogues* are poems of their time, reflecting with their quiet country background the war-weariness which was now universal.

One of these *Eclogues* deserves a special mention because Vergil gained from it a vast reputation in Christian times. It is a prophecy of a child who is to be born and under whose rule a golden age will set in. The language is exalted, raising the question of whether Vergil or one of his teachers may not have been familiar with Isaiah. In fact, however, there is no chance of the poem being a prophecy of Christ. It is possible that the child may have been the one expected by Octavian, which turned out to be a girl. It may quite likely have been that of Antony and Octavia, also a girl. In any case, our picture of Vergil is apt to be strangely colored by a coincidence which merely means that the world was longing for peace. In Palestine and Italy alike, men dreamed of a savior.

Among his friends by this time, Vergil numbered a remarkable minister of Octavian. Maecenas, aristocratic though not Roman by birth, was one of the new people in power. Polished in manner and tireless in negotiation, he was the great diplomat of the age. He was also its great literary patron. His apparently was the conception that literature should lead the way in the new era. Past glories, fresh ideals should be put before men's imaginations by great artists. Poetry should have a message for the times.

With such a purpose in mind, Maecenas found in Vergil a perfect instrument. The success of the *Eclogues* had been enormous. They were set to music and sung in the theater. Vergil was the poet of the day. Devoted to the new regime, a lover of peace and old-fashioned virtues, Italian rather than Roman, he was fitted to blend the past with the future. Accordingly, it was at the suggestion of Maecenas that, while Octavian was laboring to restore Italian agriculture, Vergil went to work on the *Georgics*, poems of farming.

These are four long, beautiful poems, of which the last about beekeeping is perhaps the most famous. Farming to Vergil is practical and hardworking. It is, however, not a mere trade, but a manner of life. Vergil sees the farmer as a whole, entering with sympathy into his relationship with nature, peopling the country with the small, familiar gods the farmer knew. The *Georgics* are polished poems, for Vergil was a slow writer, a perfectionist. It took him seven years to complete them, during which time his friendship with Maecenas blossomed. Always liberal, Maecenas gave him a villa in his own princely grounds at Rome, hoping to tempt him thither. Vergil occupied it seldom, for he did not like the city. The intimacy between the two men was great, however. It was Vergil who introduced to Maecenas the poet Horace.

Horace, a different nature from Vergil, was also of different extraction. Born in south Italy, he was of uncertain descent because his father was a freed slave who may have come from anywhere. Such a man would take over the first two names of his former master, adding to them a third one of his own, in this case Flaccus. It means "Flap-ears" and may have been his slave name, though in fact it also was a Roman surname. Flaccus's position was a very humble one. Even if freed slaves became rich, they were never considered equal with the free-born. Horace's father was of modest means. Clerk to a tax-collector or auctioneer, he also owned a little land on which he raised enough for a sparse living. The family was small. Horace's mother must have died when he was quite young, since his earliest memories are of a nurse. The father, however, more than made up for the loss. Completely devoted to his vivacious, dark-eyed son, Flaccus was proud of his talents and determined to give him a chance. When the time came for Horace to go to school, it would have been awkward to send him to the local one. The district had been settled twenty years before by the veterans of Sulla's army. The rich boys were the sons of

old centurions, tough people who no doubt thought freed
slaves should keep their place. Since Horace was undersized,
he would have been bullied and perhaps driven out of the
school. At all events, Flaccus would not expose him to such
a treatment. Collecting what must have been his very mea-
gre resources, he actually moved to Rome, where he enrolled his son in the best school he could discover.

In some respects, this presented further problems. Dress
and appearance were important if Horace was to pass
among his fellows. The ancients had a healthy respect for a
boy's power of getting into mischief if he were ever alone.
Besides, undoubtedly the streets of Rome were not very
safe. At all events, the boys were escorted to school by their
attendant slaves who carried their equipment and either
waited or returned for them. Lest Horace should seem to be
different from the rest, his father undertook the task of playing the slave, walking with him daily to and from school.
Horace, who never forgot his father's devotion, also enjoyed
his company. Intelligent, funny, and interested in people, he
seems to have found the same sort of qualities in Flaccus
during those years when they were so often together.

The school was a famous one for its severe discipline,
even in days when masters were free with the rod. No
doubt, however, the teaching was better than Vergil's. Horace, whose nature was easygoing and cheerful, made the
most of it and presumably did well. By the time he was
twenty, his indomitable father had scraped together money
for as good a higher education as any young Roman aristocrat enjoyed. Like them, Horace went to Greece — and not

just anywhere cheap, but to the eternal center of Greek culture. He went to Athens.

This was in 45 B.C., at a moment when the Civil Wars were apparently over, leaving Caesar unchallenged master. During his schooldays, Horace must have heard many a political argument as the fortunes of men swayed this way or that. Unlike Vergil, he had no particular connection with Caesar, coming as he did from a district which was loyal to Pompey. On the other hand, he seems to have had no ambition to mix himself up in politics at all. He was simply studying in Athens, just possibly finding the school of philosophy there not too sympathetic to his own practical nature. Meanwhile, in Rome, Caesar was murdered. Brutus and Cassius, yielding place to Antony, left Rome and came out East to raise an army. Cassius went to Syria for this purpose. Brutus, however, arrived in Greece and went to Athens.

Brutus at this time was just over forty and an impressive figure. Earnest, handsome, highly cultured, of a rectitude which even in those sceptical times was never questioned, he presented in his own person an idealized picture of the Republic. Arriving in Athens, he paid sincere respect to the place, went to lectures just like everybody else, and put on no airs. This behavior generated hot enthusiasm among the students. Brutus's primary business was recruiting, and he needed officers. He was even willing to offer an obscure freedman's son a commission. In a whirl of excitement, Horace joined up and was swept into the wars.

His military career ended a year or so later at the battle of Philippi, where Brutus and Cassius were killed. The defeated army fled, and Horace ran with the rest. He was not important enough to be specially persecuted, but neither had he been overlooked. He made his way back to Rome eventually to find his prospects poor. His father was dead, his little patrimony swept away by confiscation. Any friends he might possess were out of favor. He would have to see what he could do for himself.

If Horace had really felt Republican fervor, he had evidently lost it by now. Army life may have disillusioned him. In any case, he was another of those people to whom the old regime had little to offer. Making the best of things, he bought himself a situation as clerk in the Treasury, having evidently not quite exhausted his resources. Unwilling, however, to settle for a life of drudgery, he began to write poetry, hoping to attract the notice of a patron.

This may at first sight seem an unworthy motive for producing great poetry. Horace, however, would almost certainly have written in any case. In his present dilemma, he naturally turned to what he could do well. His early poems, miscellaneous and experimental, are more promising than completely successful. They served, however, to attract notice. The writing world was small, while Horace himself was excellent company. Very shortly he was introduced to Vergil, whom he always dearly loved. In turn, Vergil recommended him to Maecenas as a poet whom it might be worth his while to encourage.

It was a snobbish age, and the son of a freedman was hardly an expected guest at the house of a noble who was in confidential terms with the head of the State. Undoubtedly also, everyone who could write a bad poem pestered Maecenas, whose interest in literature was well known. For these reasons, the interview did not seem to have gone well. Horace, who was far too fond of his father to feel the slightest shame at his origin, frankly confessed this, admitting also that he had fought under Brutus. Maecenas listened, sent him away, and for nearly a year made no movement to pursue the acquaintance. Perhaps he had simply been busy, or possibly he was in a leisurely way making some inquiries. At all events, he sent for Horace long after the young man had given up hope and invited him to become one of his circle of friends. Horace's fortune — a modest one — was now made. Maecenas really liked him, and so incidentally did the emperor Augustus, who must have often relaxed at his minister's table. For Horace, apart from being a poet, was good company. He enjoyed a party and must have been uproariously funny. The humor of earlier ages is often impossible to transmit. Tastes change for one thing, and for another the suddenness of a joke and its topicality are of its essence. In time, both are lost. Thus if today we smile gently at some of Horace's sketches, his first audience must literally have held their sides.

Perhaps most typical of Horace are the poems called *Satires* which he published about the time of the defeat of Antony. Modern satire is generally a bitter thing written in anger, and with it Horace's idea of a satire has little in common. The poems really are clever sketches, written in a chatty style about anything which comes into the poet's head. He talks of his father, for instance, or about a famous journey he made with Maecenas on which Vergil joined them. We learn surprising details, such as that Maecenas went off to take some exercise at a game of ball; but that Horace had weak eyes and Vergil a delicate stomach, so they did not join him. Or at another time Horace gives a vivid sketch of a bore he says he met or lectures us on conduct, lashing out a little at obnoxious types, but always with good humor. These are poems as far removed from Vergil's as they could be, and yet the two poets have certain things in common — moral standards and a deep interest in the world around them.

It was even before the publication of the *Satires* that Maecenas had given Horace a nice little farm in the Sabine hills, complete with tenants, a slave or two and everything needed for modest country living. Seldom has any present ever given such pleasure. Like Vergil, Horace was tired of Rome. To be sure, the city stimulated him and always would; but his position must have been getting uncomfortable. He was too intimate with Augustus and his friends. Too many people tried to pump Horace dry of political secrets. In fact, Horace did not talk about politics at Maecenas's table. He had no axe to grind. Augustus asked him to become his personal secretary and help him with his private correspondence. No one with a spark of ambition would have refused. Horace, however, made his indifferent health an excuse and continued to enjoy the friendship of the Emperor, who undoubtedly appreciated the disinterestedness of the refusal.

From all such problems Horace was free in the country.

Here he really relaxed. Like Vergil, he had not married. He adored flirtations, however, and parties, and good wine. Apt to write on anything which came into his head, he produced a good many love poems. Their tone is revealing. Horace never is desperately in love, but is simply reveling in the affair. If the lady smiles, why, this is delightful. If she does not, Horace may flit off tomorrow to somebody else. Short, prematurely gray, and getting tubby, he was not the type of a romantic lover.

It was not only parties that he enjoyed in the country. The whole life suited him. He liked being able to read in bed till noon or to take a siesta beside a pretty little stream. His informal meals were attended by no more than three slaves. His rural neighbors enjoyed him without trying to get something from him.

Meantime, Maecenas and Augustus, were playfully reproaching him with the smallness of his output. He, too, had been pressed into the service of the new age. He was now writing odes, or songs in very difficult metres which he adapted with consummate skill from the Greek. Many of these were political in subject, celebrating the defeat of Cleopatra, the grandeur of Rome, the ideal citizen. Others were light and playful although sensitive to the contrast between the beauty of nature and man's short life. These brilliant poems have justly been favorites through the ages. Horace likes to portray himself as a lazy man, but the *Odes* give him the lie. It sometimes happens that a line of poetry has an inevitable quality. Its perfection lies not necessarily in what it says, but in the fact that this idea seems to have been meant to be expressed this way. No change of word could be for the better; no translation can render its effect. Such lines are rare. They do not come by instinct, but by polishing and cutting, like a jewel. The *Odes* of Horace contain as many such expressions as any other body of verse of comparable size.

While Horace was working on the *Odes*, Vergil was silent. He had already dedicated himself to the task which took up the rest of his life. His great epic, the *Aeneid*, is a hymn to the glory of Rome. Avoiding with sure instinct a historical work, he had carried himself far back into the legendary past, reviving that unconvincing legend which traced the ancestry of Caesar to Aeneas, child of a goddess and hero of Troy. This invested his work at the start with the glamour of Homer, and Vergil was not afraid to imitate his model in what at times seems an almost slavish way. Achilles celebrates elaborate funeral games. Aeneas does likewise. The shield of Achilles and that of Aeneas both have pictures which are described at length. Since Odysseus consults the spirits of the dead, why, so must Aeneas. Yet these resemblances are only superficial. The shield of Aeneas contains a prophetic picture of Octavian's victory. In the underworld, Aeneas meets the shadows of the heroes, as yet unborn, who will glorify Rome. The very fighting is not on the plains of Troy, but in the Italy which Vergil knew so well. Odysseus wanders quite simply to get home. Aeneas is the servant of destiny, fated to found a glorious city, committed to a future greater than himself. Into this poem Vergil poured all his feelings of patriotism, love of nature, compassion for man. In 19 B.C. he had been working on it for twelve years; and none was published, though he had read sections to Augustus. Vergil was unwilling to call it finished. It was unworthy of his conception as yet, but he intended to improve it. In the meantime, whether for recreation or research, he went to Greece.

It happened at that moment that Augustus was returning from a long tour in the East and that he also came through Greece on his way home. Naturally the two met, for they were friends; and Augustus suggested that they go together and examine the ruins of Megara. The day was extremely hot; and Vergil, whose health as we know was always poor, fell ill as a result. Augustus, unwilling to abandon him in Greece, took him home by the easiest stages he could contrive; but it was hopeless. When they landed in Italy at Brundisium, Vergil was dying.

What distressed him most of all was the unfinished "Aeneid." To his sick fancy it was not adequate, and he called for his manuscript in order to destroy it. When he could not obtain it, he enjoined his friends as his dying wish to burn it. Augustus, however, had heard at least part of the poem and knew its worth. He forbade its destruction and had it published forthwith. It established Vergil as one of the great poets of the ages.

The death of Vergil, lamented by all his friends, left Horace to be the official poet of the age. Accordingly, he was commissioned to write a song in connection with Augustus's Secular Games. These games, occurring roughly once a century, were a traditional festival at Rome and supposed to mark the beginning of a new age. They were therefore particularly suitable for Augustus, who celebrated them with much pomp. The ode of Horace, duly sung, is a poem adequate to the occasion, but perhaps no more. Horace was turning back into the style of his *Satires*, enriched by a greater maturity. Frankness, kindliness, humor were his best qualities; and he was not primarily a political poet. Yet his moral interests and his literary ones expressed themselves in his verse, setting their own stamp on his age. Maecenas could still congratulate himself on discovering Horace. Augustus continued to be his intimate friend. Both statesmen recognized his worth and his contribution. If either urged him in the later years of his life to produce more political poems, they were not successful. Probably they were content not to press him, especially as his health seemed to decline. He died, a few months later than Maecenas, at the end of 8 B.C., having produced in the last years of his life two books of *Epistles*, or letters in verse, and a poem on literary criticism of great interest. Augustus was yet to rule for twenty-two years, but the character of his age was formed. The work of the great poets who had helped to shape it was now over.

NERO *and* SENECA

Nero Claudius Caesar, A.D. 37–68
Lucius Annaeus Seneca, 4 B.C.–A.D. 65

THE Emperor Claudius, third in succession after Augustus, was descended from Octavia, Antony, and Augustus's younger stepson. He had always been despised by his family. Claudius was deformed, probably by infantile paralysis. He was thick in utterance, and he drooled. He was not, however, the half-wit people thought him. Thrust into the background, Claudius had become a learned antiquarian while the succession passed from his uncle Tiberius to his nephew Caius.

The jealousies of the imperial house, which had led to many deaths, passed Claudius by. The Emperor Caius, however, was an irresponsible young man who soon showed signs of mental aberration. Physically timid, inarticulate, clumsy, poor Claudius was the ideal victim of crude jokes. Luckily for him, Caius was shortly murdered by a group of officers who found his vagaries intolerable.

The act unleashed chaos in Rome. There was now no obvious heir to the imperial throne. The Emperor's private guard invaded the palace, leaderless, with an eye to loot, cutting down the late Emperor's friends. Ineffectually

Claudius tried to hide behind a curtain. Somebody pulled him out. The soldiers, partly as a joke, but partly because there was nobody else, saluted him as Emperor. They carried him on their shoulders away to their camp.

In this undignified way the uncouth Claudius was proclaimed Emperor. Surprisingly, he proved to be a good one. His personal qualities, however, obscured his virtues, particularly in Rome. In matters of policy, Claudius might be intelligent, but he had no experience of administrative detail. He entrusted his business to trained servants, freedmen with an eye to their own advantage. Corruption ran rampant. Worse still, the greed of the freedmen was equaled by that of Claudius's wife.

Messalina, young, beautiful, well born, had been married to her elderly, unattractive husband in the usual Roman way, without much consideration for her views. Against all expectation, she found herself wife to an emperor. Her situation went to her head. Claudius was indulgent, absent-minded, and gullible. Messalina embarked on a course which could only end in scandal. When it did so, she lost her life and Claudius his illusions.

He would have been wise to stay unmarried, especially since he had a son and heir. He was, however, surrounded by ambitious ladies openly competing for the position of consort. Unworldly, domestic in tastes, Claudius was no match for them. The prize was eventually carried off by Agrippina, the Emperor's own niece, who proved the most determined and unscrupulous of the claimants.

Agrippina on her father's side was descended from the

same stock as Claudius himself. Her mother, however, an older Agrippina, had been daughter to Julia and Marcus Agrippa. In Agrippina's veins there ran the blood of the great Augustus. She had been already married to Cnaius Domitius Ahenobarbus, a cousin of the imperial family, by whom she had one son. It was rumored that she had poisoned her husband for his money. In the absence of any evidence, however, we may give Agrippina some benefit of the doubt, merely remarking that she was quite capable of it. At the time she married Claudius, she was thirty-four years old and he fifty-nine. Energetic, insatiable in ambition, she rapidly domineered over her elderly husband, directing her intrigues toward securing the throne for her son in preference to his.

Young Domitius Ahenobarbus was twelve at this time, a good-looking boy with red-gold curls and showy talents. Claudius's own son, Britannicus, was only seven. Agrippina scored a coup by appointing as her son's tutor the philosopher Seneca, most famous literary figure of the age. The appointment recalled, as it was meant to do, how the young Alexander the Great was tutored by Aristotle. Claudius was next persuaded to advance the date at which Ahenobarbus put on the dress of a man. This brought him into the limelight while Britannicus was still in the schoolroom. Agrippina had persuaded the doting old man that her son would act as guardian for the younger boy. Claudius, who felt himself growing feeble, was foolish enough to adopt Ahenobarbus and give him the hand of his daughter Octavia in marriage. The boy now, as the custom was, took names belonging to his new father, Nero Claudius Germanicus. He was known as Nero.

All these arrangements were complete by the time that Agrippina was five years married. There was no point in waiting any longer for the old man to die. Sooner or later Britannicus must put on the dress of a man and would appear as a rival for the succession. Agrippina, or so the historians say, poisoned her husband with a dish of mushrooms. Possibly this is not true, but at all events, Claudius died. Agrippina had already consolidated her position by an alliance with the most powerful of the freedmen. Young Nero, an attractive boy and much in the public eye, was a descendant of Augustus, which Britannicus was not. He had been brought forward by Claudius himself. Of course he succeeded.

The reign began with a great outburst of goodwill. The young Emperor, adopted by Claudius and married to his daughter, was welcomed by the provinces and by the frontier legions with whom Claudius had been justly popular. In Rome itself, the contrast between the grotesque figure of the late Emperor and the handsome boy of seventeen was striking. The timidity of Claudius and the ambitions of his freedmen or wives had led to intrigues in which prominent figures had been victimized. Paid informers had flourished. Obscure persons of foreign extraction had been raised to high positions, while the authority and prestige of the Senate had diminished. All these evils would now, it was felt, be corrected. The reputation of the tutor Seneca was high, and it was evident that the administration would be in his hands.

His colleague, an elderly man named Burrus who commanded the powerful imperial guard, had been a trusted counselor for three reigns. Agrippina, it is true, was not liked. She had, however, gained her object and might be expected to be content with it. Nero, prompted by his advisers, was displaying great modesty. He refused the title of "Father of his Country," declined to have his statue put up, deferred to the Senate, and seemed to model himself on the young Augustus. These tactics pleased all alike. Affection and flattery were poured out in unlimited quantities on him.

Lucius Annaeus Seneca, to whom the government of the next five years was to be due, was a man of brilliant though distorted talents. He was born in Spain and of Spanish extraction, but his father had spent much time in Rome. His mother, Helvia, had a sister living there, to whom the boy was entrusted when quite young. He owed his life to her care, since he was always ailing. Her influence started him on an official career. In preparation for this, he had studied rhetoric in the usual way, acquiring also, somewhat to his father's dismay, a passion for philosophy which was to prove lifelong.

The Stoic philosophy was the real religion of the Roman aristocrat in these days. It concerned itself largely with ethical questions. The aim of the wise man was to live in harmony with nature. Nature, however, is guided by reason, or God. To live by the light of reason is the only good thing in life. If a man does so, he is independent of good or evil fortune. Pain, death, suffering have no terrors for him. Pleasure is no temptation. He remains above such things, master of his own soul and content with this inner kingdom.

This is a philosophy of life particularly suited to those who have lost control of their own fate. Deprived of power, the Roman aristocrat was forced to put up with acts of which he could not approve. Exposed by his prominence to the fear of emperors or the intrigues of their servants, he too often perished for crimes in which he had no share. A philosophy which taught him that the mere events of life were unimportant suited his needs.

Of this philosophy Seneca became a devotee. Eager and imaginative, he soon varied his law-court speeches with tracts on ethical subjects and by dramas based on the old classical models but up-dated to please the modern taste. Seneca's writing is a model of his mind. His dramas, for instance, are a curious mixture of crude sensationalism and moral lecture. In a tired generation, Seneca is compelled to be shocking and clever. Their dramatic qualities are highly colored ones. He has a gift for purple passages of description, but little for dialogue or character presentation. His own brilliance concerns him, but not that of others. His people are types.

In his prose works he shows the same qualities with an added worldly wisdom which may seem curious in a professed Stoic. Seneca, in fact, is having the best of both worlds. He feels superior to the life around him, but he is not. The force behind his ethics is emotional, not intellectual. His writings are born of a craving to be admired. In fact, he is the possessor of a demanding ego which

is bolstered up by his pretensions. He does not care for too close logical thought. His aspirations are genuine enough in the sense that he feels them, but they do not necessarily control his life.

With such conspicuous qualities, Seneca was soon the fashion. His moral ideals gave him a reputation which his wit and rhetoric enhanced. By the late thirties when Caius succeeded to the throne, he was established as the first orator and poet in town. It was a reputation which nearly proved fatal to him. The megalomania of Caius could not endure any kind of rivalry. It was only the emperor's timely murder which saved Seneca.

Unfortunately for him he soon fell victim to the intrigues of Claudius's wife Messalina. He was banished on an improbable charge and we are left to speculate how he had managed to insinuate himself at all into such circles. He retired to Corsica, where his behavior was not stoic. He went so far as to publish a cringing address to one of the Emperor's conspicuous freedmen, but in vain. He was not recalled until the influence of Agrippina brought him back as tutor to her son.

His behavior on the accession of Nero was as ambivalent as might be expected. The prudent modesty of the new emperor was a tribute to his advice. Yet Seneca must still have the best of both worlds. For the purpose of pleasing the provinces, Claudius was pronounced a god. But to please sophisticated Rome, Seneca published a skit called "The Pumpkinification of Claudius" which was exceedingly vulgar, impudently funny, an open mockery of the dead Emperor himself and the state religion.

Such was the chief minister of Nero. It seemed, however, as though the real ruler at first was Agrippina, who had attained a special position as "Augusta and Mother of Augustus." She was even able to cause the Senate to leave their meetinghouse, which she as a woman could not enter, and adjourn to the Palatine, where she could listen to their debates. Nero, meanwhile, devoted himself with fervor to the arts. Presently, however, a lack of balance in his character began to give cause for serious concern. He became the center of a young, dissipated set whose irregular love affairs and midnight escapades in the town were causing scandal. Agrippina remonstrated, only to discover that her son was no longer under her thumb. High words passed between them. Agrippina did not hesitate to say that she had made an Emperor and could unmake one. Britannicus was already too old for the schoolroom. She would set him up, if she cared to do so, in her son's place.

Such an outburst can only have been intended to frighten Nero into obedience. It resulted, however, in the murder of Britannicus. Undoubtedly this would have been a moment for Seneca and Burrus, who were ruling in Nero's name, to think their position over. If a young man of eighteen could resort to murder to suit his convenience, how long should upright men continue to guide his affairs? However, the curious, disingenuous character of Seneca always allowed him to reconcile his high moral standards with ambition. He was already at odds with Agrippina, whose defeat by her son would make it possible for Seneca to push her aside. Meanwhile things were going well, on the whole. The regime was popular. If Seneca resigned, things would change for the worse.

For reasons such as these, Seneca and Burrus passed over the murder of Britannicus. They disregarded, too, the developing character of Nero, since this was convenient to them. They profited from his dislike of administrative work. All the same, they dared not let him undermine his own position to the point of jeopardizing the regime. Conflict centered about the figure of Octavia, Nero's wife and Britannicus's sister. Nero's marriage to this lady, as generally beloved as her earlier namesake, had been a major cause of his accession. Ill-feeling soon resulted from his open neglect. As long, however, as Nero's flame of the moment was a freedwoman whom he could not deign to marry, poor Octavia remained in name his wife. Unhappily, he soon fell in love with Poppaea Sabina, a famous beauty and wife of one of his dissolute companions. She aspired to be his consort. Seneca, Burrus, and Agrippina herself were driven to protest. It would be dangerous for Nero to put aside the late Emperor's daughter.

In face of such opposition, Nero dared not do what he desired. He was surrounded, however, by those who were teaching him that he need put up with no restraint. Poppaea herself was urgent with him to seize power. In consequence, a mere five years after his accession, Nero was induced to plot the murder of his mother. Still afraid of her in a way, he went to the most elaborate lengths to stage an accident. Pretending a reconciliation, he quelled her suspicions by a display of the affection that she craved. He actually lent her his yacht for a short trip. This, however, had been secretly built in such a way that it could be made to fall apart, thus drowning — or so it was hoped — both Agrippina and all the witnesses to the accident.

The affair took place, but not quite as planned. The vessel was not far enough out; and Agrippina, though struck by a falling block, was not disabled. She swam ashore. Here her position was pitiable indeed. It was quite obvious to her what her son had attempted. She was both terrified and cut to the heart. Immediately she sent him a message which was meant to assure him that she had no suspicions. It threw Nero into a panic. He knew his mother could not have been deceived. There was nothing for it but to accuse her of having made an attempt on his life. On this pretext, men were hastily despatched to kill her, which they did clumsily and without concealing their orders.

Seneca and Burrus were by this time so enmeshed in palace intrigue that they connived at Nero's murder of his mother. Seneca's scruples had been growing less and less, so that he actually composed the explanation which Nero gave to the Senate. His complacence secured him a few years of nominal power. Eventually, however, Burrus died. Nero replaced him with a corrupt creature of his own. Deprived of the guard's support and nearing seventy, Seneca became anxious to retire. He was, however, frightened to do so. Though he claimed a mind above worldly things, he had used his position to accumulate vast wealth. Indeed it is said that the rebellion in Britain which took place during the reign was caused by the activities of Seneca's agents operating as moneylenders and reducing the province to misery as a result of their extortions. Seneca offered his treasure to Nero now, thinking it safer. Nero, however, in this instance was not to be bribed. He refused the present, and Seneca is said to have seen his death warrant in this.

Nero had already started to live as he pleased. Divorcing Octavia, he trumped up a charge of adultery and sent her to a barren island, where she remained until he felt secure enough to send executioners. He married Poppaea, and the two embarked on wild extravagance. Poppaea, whose beauty was her chief hold over Nero, would not travel without a vast herd of she-asses who were milked for her bath. The size of her retinue was fabulous. Nero for his part made expensive efforts to set up athletic games and musical contests as rivals to the popular gladiatorial shows. A more serious character might have won some respect for his views, but the frivolity of Nero was shocking. Eager to display his accomplishments, he built a private circus where he raced as charioteer. Similarly, he appeared on a stage of his own, both in tragedies and musical recitals. These demonstrations became gradually more public, requiring groups of spectators trained beforehand to lead the applause. Since entertainers in Nero's day were of the lowest classes, his behavior affected public opinion rather as though the Queen of England were to insist on starring in striptease.

Affairs of state, meanwhile, were once more being entrusted to low-born, unscrupulous people. Extravagance had emptied the treasury. A rebellion in Britain and a war in Armenia compelled Nero to debase the coinage. Treason trials of prominent people started anew, and it became evident that the confiscation of property from the rich was a temptation to Nero. Meanwhile, his most distant connections soon fell victim to his insane suspicions.

A couple of years after Seneca's fall, Nero's popularity had reached a low ebb. The Senate might have condoned the murder of his mother and Seneca might have excused it, but the public conscience had been genuinely shocked. Nero's treatment of Octavia caused further outrage, as did his private behavior. A misfortune with which he had nothing to do now demonstrated that people were ready to believe any evil of him.

Nero was actually on holiday in the country when a fire, breaking out in the Circus Maximus, raged for nine days and laid half Rome in ruins. Returning with all speed, Nero directed crews of firefighters, threw open the grounds of his palace to refugees, saw to the erection of huts and tents, and imported cheap food. In short, he did what he could. A story, however, went about that the fire had been set at his orders so that he might see what a burning city looked like. It was also said that he had watched the conflagration from a safe place, while reciting a description of burning Troy which happened to be part of a poem he had composed himself.

This legend, which slowly gained ground, was fed by resentment at Nero's later proceedings. Again, in a sense, he

did what he could. Presented by fortune with an opportunity to display artistic gifts, he attempted to rise to the
occasion. Architects were commissioned to plan Rome on
more modern lines. Nero collected forced contributions
from the provinces for rebuilding Rome, denuded Greece of
art treasures to adorn it, and gave subsidies to builders. But
he also took advantage of the devastation to build himself a
Golden House whose extravagance and size were purely fan-
tastic. It contained whole parks, lakes and woods. One of its
three colonnades extended a mile. The roof of one of its
banqueting rooms was made to open so that flowers could
be rained down on the guests. Its vestibule contained a
statue of Nero a hundred and twenty feet high. A building of
this kind was a vast insult to those who had suffered from
the fire. Eventually even Nero realized that something must
be done to quiet public opinion. Needing scapegoats to
blame for setting the fire, he chose the Christians.

The position of the Christians in the Roman world at this
point needs explaining. Emperor-worship, which was by
now a general obligation, was never confused with the worship of real gods. It was merely a way of expressing loyalty.
It therefore annoyed people when the Jews regarded these
two forms of worship as one. There was, however, some
excuse for Jews maintaining that emperor-worship violated
their beliefs, since the Jewish religion had been established
long before Augustus. The Christians, on the other hand,
were a new sect. They were, moreover, a sect which actually
did worship a man and could not therefore claim that this
was against their principles. It could be nothing but disloy-

alty, people felt, which made them refuse to worship the Emperor also. To this may be added the fact that eastern religions were widely regarded in Rome — not always without justice — as degrading. At regular intervals some scandal or other would induce the government to expel such sects from Rome and to punish their adherents. In fact, Christianity, encouraged by the presence of Peter and Paul in Rome at this time, was beginning to be heard of by people who knew nothing of its doctrines and readily assumed the worst.

The persecution of the Christians by Nero was for these reasons not condemned by many people. The general feeling was that they deserved their fate. To be sure, Nero's party given by the light of human torches, and his wholesale crucifixions were more drastic than the usual punishment of foreign sectaries. But a populace used to gladiatorial shows was not refined in its feelings. It was not the innocence of the victims thrown to the lions which outraged the Roman people, but the hypocrisy of the hated Nero. His proceedings merely fixed the guilt on him more firmly than ever.

The rapid development of Nero's viciousness had brought out, not for the first time, a weakness of the Empire. It was only too true that the ruler could do what he liked. If he cared to make his three-months-old dead baby a goddess he could do so. When he kicked Poppaea in a fit of drunken anger, bringing on a miscarriage from which she died, no one could touch him. When thereafter he desired to make Poppaea a goddess, too, she became one. In fact, for all his care in concealing it, Augustus had established a military dictatorship. Commanding the loyalty of the legions and the imperial guard, an emperor could not be controlled. In the hands of Augustus, this absolute power had done good. In lesser characters like Caius and Nero, it developed an insane selfishness and vanity. When this happened, the only method of reform was revolution. It was not long after the fall of Seneca that serious people saw the necessity of getting rid of Nero. A conspiracy was formed among the more energetic of the better class. As usual, however, the positive side of the plot was far less easy to agree upon than the negative one. Most inclined to make an emperor out of Calpurnius Piso, a distinguished and amiable man who seems to have been chosen for the insufficient reason that everyone liked him. Others inclined to Seneca, who, though old, had actually ruled and was known throughout the Empire.

The plot very nearly succeeded, but the conspirators made the mistake of letting too many into their secret. On the very day before the assassination was to have taken place, two men were denounced who, under torture, confessed and named accomplices. Exposure followed.

The fear and rage of Nero may be imagined. The mere conspiracy was bad enough, but the distinguished roster of its members was a disaster. From now onward, Nero never dared trust the very people who governed his provinces or commanded his armies. Naturally his vengeance fell heavily on the accused. To avoid sensational trials, he ordered many to commit suicide. By leaving fulsome letters of praise for the Emperor and by naming him beneficiary of their wills, such people hoped at least to save the lives of their families and reserve a small part of their fortunes.

Seneca was denounced by only one man, but his fate was certain. An order for suicide was sent to him. There is no doubt Seneca had condoned some very great crimes through fear, and he had lost the respect of the best people. Now, however, when the inevitable came, he faced it with dignity. Following what had become the fashionable procedure, he called on his doctor to open the veins of his wrists. His wife Paulina, many years younger than he, insisted on dying with him. Seneca, however, was old; and perhaps the doctor bungled. At all events, the blood did not flow as it should. The old man tried to hasten the process by a hot bath, but in vain. Eventually, after hours of suffering, he died. By Nero's order, Paulina's wrists were bound up and she was nursed back to life.

Her escape was an exceptional one, for Nero's suspicions soon ranged beyond the original members of the plot. Both Seneca's brothers now died and his nephew Lucan, the poet. Even former friends of Nero fell victim to his jealousies. The most distinguished of these, Petronius, known as the Arbiter of Elegance, was a brilliant but dissipated man who had long presided disdainfully over Nero's curious mixture of vulgar sensationalism and amateur culture. He at least died no servile death. Sitting at a banquet while his life bled away, he insisted on occasions on having his wrists bound up, so that he might enter more fully into the conversation. Meanwhile, he is said to have entertained his frightened companions by his whole, unexpurgated opinion of Nero. Finally with his dying hand he smashed the priceless Greek vases which he knew Nero chiefly coveted.

No distinguished man now felt his life safe. The situation bred a conspiracy once more, this time involving not the Senators at Rome but the generals on the frontier. Even Nero was forced to have recourse to strategy before he could order the deaths of Corbulo, most famous soldier of his age, and of the Scribonii who were the commanders of the Upper and Lower German frontiers. These, however, were fatal acts. During his principate, Nero had never showed himself to his armies. Their loyalty, which was to their generals, was rudely shaken. Other generals likewise trembled for their futures. Nero meanwhile was occupied in publicly affronting the ideas of majesty throughout the Empire.

He had long desired to make a tour of Greece. To his inflamed vanity, he was a supreme musical artist; and he craved recognition in the land of athletic games and musical contests. Accordingly, accompanied by a vast retinue, he made his way thither to quarter himself for nearly a year on its impoverished cities to whom he grandiloquently gave "freedom," by which he meant a local autonomy and a remission of tribute. These were privileges which aroused bitter envy in other provinces which had been lately oppressed by forced contributions toward the rebuilding of Rome. Nero, however, disregarding the effect of his lavishness, proceeded to compete in the Greek games. Every city put on some sort of festival for him, while the Olympian, the Isthmian, and other traditional games were all celebrated in one year. Nero displayed himself from end to end of Greece as charioteer, poet, orator, and singer, taking each occasion with the utmost seriousness, despite the fact that of course he always won. Indeed, he actually won on many occasions when he did not even compete and thus was able to dedicate on his return over eighteen hundred wreaths of laurel or wild olive or whatever more lavish type of triumphal crown the cities provided.

This ludicrous display on Nero's part, far more public in the eyes of the Empire at large than his proceedings in Italy, lost him respect. While he was appearing in men's and women's parts on the public stage, his soldiers were fighting a serious war in Judea without him. At the same time, his favors to Greece stimulated local ambition in other provinces to have privilege likewise. The first sign of trouble was a revolt in Gaul, in itself serious, yet quickly suppressed with the aid of the Rhine armies. Next Galba, Roman commander of Further Spain, threw off allegiance to Nero and declared himself subject only to the Senate. The Empire was breaking up at its extremities. Important generals, from Galba in the West to Vespasian, engaged in putting down the rebellion of the Jews, saw no reason to wait tamely for the fate of Corbulo. All possible connections of the imperial house had been exterminated. There was no claimant to the throne and therefore each general could back himself.

Disasters piled up fast. If Nero had had a spark of sense, he still might have conquered. The magic of the Julian name was great. Naturally, however, he did the wrong things, alienating everybody by his lack of commonsense. There was, for instance, a food shortage in Rome. When ships came into the harbor, they were seen to be full of sand for the erection of a public stage for more displays of Nero. At last the guard revolted. Nero, attempting to flee, perceived he was caught. Nothing remained for him but suicide, and his attendants urged this on him as the only possible way out. He saw this himself, but could not make up his mind. "What an artist will be lost to the world in me!" he exclaimed in agony. At last, however, he called on his freedman to help him and with his aid drove in the sword. The pursuers — so late had he left it — burst in immediately and found him dying. He was only thirty years old.

Thus perished the last of the Julian Caesars, less than fifty years after the death of great Augustus, after running the gamut of depravity and vice. The prize of Empire was now up for the strongest man, and it remained to be seen what dynasty would follow.

TRAJAN

Marcus Ulpius Traianus, A.D. 53–117

THE dynasty of the Flavians, which established itself after the death of Nero, faced the task of restoring public confidence. The death of the last Julian emperor had been followed by civil wars in which various army commanders were put forward by their own troops. There seemed grave danger that the Empire would be torn apart by these struggles and that any stability which the system of Augustus had possessed might be destroyed forever. Luckily, the three Flavian emperors were energetic, experienced men who showed themselves capable of maintaining their power. The frontier system was reorganized; the armies were brought under control; the worst abuses of Nero's degenerate regime were corrected. All these valuable services, however, were not enough to reconcile the Romans to the character of the third Flavian, Domitian.

They detested, in the first place, his arrogance. A man of great ambition, Domitian aspired to be not the first citizen of Rome, but her absolute monarch. Men were forced to prostrate themselves before him, kiss his hands or his feet. Domitian was too lordly even to dine with his own guests,

while conversation at his evening receptions seemed to consist in everyone taking turns to speak in praise of the emperor. Domitian merely listened in grim silence, hardly deigning to utter a word, even of acknowledgment.

Along with these manners went a complete disregard of Senate and council. Augustus, though he gathered real power into his own hands, had respected the Senate. He had asked its advice and had followed it. He had used its members to govern provinces, command armies, and head the departments of state. Under Domitian, the time of the Senate was taken up with voting him titles or statues with honorific inscriptions. The satirist Juvenal, writing after Domitian's death, gives a fanciful picture of him summoning his council of state to advise him on how to cook a very large fish which had been presented to him. The occasion is not a real one, but it sums up neatly the arrogance of the man and the trivial matters which he condescended to lay before his advisers.

Domitian had come to the throne in middle age, postponed for many years to his older brother. The treatment had soured him. He knew himself to be disliked and saw disloyalty in slight and even unconscious offenses. The inefficient governor of a province, the injudicious army commander perished for treason. The man who stayed away from the Senate on the day on which it voted an address to Domitian for his birthday did so likewise. The man who was related to the old imperial house; Domitian's own favorites, grown too powerful; his successful generals, grown too prominent, all died. Nor did the tyrant confine his suspicions to important people. The poet Juvenal was a young man of respectable Italian stock and some means, eager to start on a public career. He gave Domitian offense, apparently by referring to the corrupt power of a former favorite who had been put to death by his master ten years earlier. One might have imagined that it was safe to allude to the misdoings of a man whom the Emperor himself had condemned. Domitian, however, chose to interpret the poet's words as a criticism. Juvenal's fortune was confiscated and he himself was banished to a remote village on the borders of Egypt.

Things came to a point in Rome where no one's life seemed safe. Domitian's murder, desired by so many, was finally accomplished by a conspiracy in which his own wife and the captain of his palace guard took part. It was followed by open public rejoicing. Hated statues were hastily torn down, inscriptions defaced. It was recognized, however, that a serious crisis existed. The Flavian dynasty, like the Julian, had come to an end. Was the death of Domitian to be followed by civil war like that of Nero?

Hastily the Senate imposed a candidate of its own, an elderly nobleman called Nerva who had a blameless record and was supported by a group of people who most of them were even older than he was. It was an uninspiring choice. Domitian, unpopular as he might have been with those who came under his eye, was liked by the soldiers serving on the frontiers. He had raised their pay and taken interest in the conditions of their service. Nerva was not a military man, and he did not have connections with Domitian's serving generals. Nor was he in a position to buy power where he could not command it. A bonus was traditionally given the soldiers by a succeeding emperor. This Nerva promised to pay, since he dared not refuse it. His difficulties, however, were great; for the treasury was empty.

Domitian, despite some grandiose building schemes, had not the extravagance of Nero. It was rather that taxes had not kept pace with increasing demand or even with the growing wealth of portions of the Empire. Domitian, who took enormous sums in confiscations from those condemned for treason, had put off unpopular reforms. The more honorable Nerva was without this source of extra supply and faced a stringency.

For all these reasons, the regime of Nerva was soon in difficulty. His personal outlook, like that of his class, was more Italian than imperial. Such needed public works as he put in hand were Italian. Italy, flooded remorselessly by slave labor, plagued by great estates and absentee landlords, really needed a thorough rehabilitation. This was not, however, a task which appealed either to the armies or to the provinces where they resided. It was only natural that opposition to Nerva began to mount.

The Palace, or Praetorian Guard, nearest to the scene of action, took the lead. These guards, higher paid and better treated than the frontier soldiers, had always been favorites of the current ruler, since his power depended on them. It was recognized that the Prefect of the Praetorian Guard was the second person in Rome. The Guard had made emperors. It had also pulled them down. Domitian had been murdered, without the Guard's consent, even though their Prefect had been concerned in the matter. Nerva had been elevated to the throne by the Senate, which had not consulted the Guard. Accordingly the troops grumbled and eventually proceeded to open revolt. They demanded from Nerva the death of the people who had murdered Domitian. To these, Nerva owed his throne. In senatorial circles, it was agreed that the deed had been a praiseworthy one. Nerva, however, had no troops. If he did not give way, it was clear that he would lose his imperial position. When he yielded, however, it became equally obvious that he could not long retain it. His power had been shown to be too shaky to protect his own best friends.

There was only one thing to be done. Nerva was elderly and in the course of events could not be expected to rule long. He was also childless. He must name his heir and must choose one who had the military strength which he lacked. Accordingly Nerva made choice of Marcus Ulpius Traianus, who was at that time commanding the Roman forces of Upper Germany, stationed on the Rhine. It was a sound choice, and it saved Nerva. About a year later Nerva performed another, final service for his country. He died, leaving behind him the greatest Roman ruler since Augustus.

Marcus Ulpius Traianus, who thus unexpectedly fell heir to the Empire was a new departure in Roman emperors altogether. Trajan was neither Roman nor yet, except in a distant way, Italian. He was Spanish.

About two hundred years before Christ, the Romans had conquered Spain in the course of their wars with Carthage.

They had immediately settled a colony of their veteran soldiers in a town they called Italica, just south of the modern Córdoba. In the next two hundred and fifty years, the descendants of these people intermarried freely with the native Spaniards, who were thoroughly Romanized. They preserved the tradition of their Italian descent, possessed Roman citizenship, and were at liberty to enter on Roman public life with little more handicap than that which Cicero had once felt on coming from Arpinum. The father of Trajan married a Spanish lady and kept up residence in Italica, where his son Trajan was born. His career, however, was a Roman one. Along with a number of other distinguished provincials, he was elevated to the Senate by Vespasian, the first Flavian Emperor, who was seeking to fill up its depleted ranks. The older Trajan served as governor of his own province, rose to the consulate, and became an administrator with wide powers in the East. This last position would have lent distinction to the noblest Senatorial family. The older Trajan with no such tradition at his back must have attained it by an ability beyond the common.

Trajan himself started his career in his father's service, accompanying him to Syria in the capacity of military tribune and serving ten years in various places in that rank. The fact is significant. The military tribune was a junior commissioned officer, superior to a centurion as a captain is to a top sergeant. It was a customary, though not a universal rank for a young Roman noble while gaining experience of military affairs. Those, however, who remained in this position for ten years were a special group. It was always possible for a young man to devote himself to the military life; but those who did so had been generally those who might rise further in the army than in the political field. Their careers had been limited by the fact that Roman generals were appointed from Senatorial ranks. A good professional could certainly count on being chosen as right-hand man to a succession of inexperienced generals. If, like Caesar, he wanted a command himself, he entered political life. This system, however, was breaking down in Trajan's day. The civil wars after the death of Nero had served to show that it was dangerous to put men in command of important armies who were of noble birth. It was too easy for such a one to aspire to be Emperor. Under the Flavians, command went rather to men like Trajan — provincials, decently connected, little known in Rome, but professional soldiers. Trajan's importance developed steadily, even under Domitian, that most suspicious of men. He did not apparently look like a feasible candidate for Empire.

The most dangerous event in Domitian's reign was a rebellion against him by Saturninus, then in command in upper Germany. The Upper German Army, though not necessarily the strongest of the Roman frontier armies, was always in the best position to threaten Rome. It was nearer than the Danube, while the Lower German Army was stationed further north on the Rhine near Cologne. The rebellion of Saturninus could very easily have been fatal to Domitian, had the commanders of the other armies failed in loyalty. Trajan, who was at this time commander of a legion in Spain, had set out to crush the revolt without hesitation. Other generals had followed suit. The rebellion had been suppressed. Domitian transferred some legions from the disaffected army and, a year or two later, rewarded Trajan's loyalty by appointing him its general.

At the time of Nerva's choice, then, Trajan was an active man of forty-four with a minimum of experience in Rome, an excellent administrator, always popular with his soldiers, and in command of a strategic army. Most of his advantages might have been supposed to weigh comparatively little with Nerva, who had other important generals to choose from, besides close kinsmen of his own. The provincial origin of Trajan must have been felt to be a drawback, by a Senator of Nerva's conventional mold. Since we do not, however, know all the practical choices available to Nerva at this moment, we cannot tell how far Trajan stood out. He did have one friend at court. Lucius Sura, also a Spaniard, was like Trajan an expert in frontier defense. The two men knew each other well. Now Sura, who was at this time in command of a legion at Bonn, was far more at home in Roman society than Trajan. Sura knew everybody, and his interest went far. There can be little doubt that his personal choice was Trajan. It seems not unlikely that he urged him on Nerva. At all events, the decision was made. Trajan was formally adopted as Nerva's son and given the title of Caesar. He did not come to Rome for these ceremonies, did not even so much as meet Nerva. He stayed on the frontier, where his influence was needed. A year later when Nerva died, the succession passed to him without the smallest hitch. Everybody had accepted the arrangement, while the

140 LIVES OF FAMOUS ROMANS

armies of the Rhine and the Danube were enthusiastic. It was not even necessary to go to Rome at once. Having urgent business on the Danube frontier, Trajan went there.

He came to Rome a year later in 98, and many people must have had their first glimpse of their new master. He made an excellent impression. Personally, Trajan was a tall, well-built man with a round bullet-head, deep eyes, strong features, and a heavy thatch of straight hair which he combed forward over his forehead. His manner was simple and direct. Avoiding all ostentation, he entered Rome on foot, thus marking his intention to behave like a citizen and not an eastern monarch.

Though very much the master, Trajan put on no airs. He was sparing in his acceptance of honorary titles, and respected the Senate's prestige. He was easy of access and ready to listen to the opinions of experts, but he made up his own mind. The combination was needed, since the Senate in truth was not fit to govern. Many of its best members had been murdered by Domitian. Of the remainder, some had risen to power by currying favor with the tyrant and preferring accusations against others. Now that their privileges were restored, the Senators asserted themselves by being far too lenient with their own members. Grave cases of provincial misgovernment were allowed to pass unpunished, and serious scandals took place. Trajan, however, knew how to deal with this in patience, offering well-timed advice or persuading the Senators to let him take over a province for a few years, sending out to it a special commissioner to put things right. To the province of Bithynia in Asia Minor, which was in serious financial difficulties, he appointed one of the best Senators of the period, the younger Pliny. The title distinguishes him from an uncle, a famous scholar who perished when the eruption of Vesuvius overwhelmed Pompeii.

It is a constant tradition of modern times that the Roman Empire was a degenerate world at best and that by the end of its first century it had already lost what virtues it might have possessed. The judgment is strengthened by the murders and scandals of the imperial house so faithfully chronicled by Tacitus, the historian, who was writing during the age of Trajan. The vitriolic poems of the satirist Juvenal reinforce this impression. According to Juvenal, no moral standards now existed. Selfish materialism had swept away even the restraints of family affection. There were no decencies left.

To read the letters of the younger Pliny, written at the same time, is to step into another world. It is peopled by high-minded, conscientious men whose family affections are strong and whose children are promising. They live in considerable luxury, but are generous with their money. Pliny had endowed his native town with a fund which makes provision for the upbringing of poor girls and boys. He recounts his methods of securing the money in perpetuity to a friend who is anxious to work out a way of doing the same thing. Of all Pliny's letters, none are more interesting than the ones he wrote from Bithynia to Trajan, which are published together with Trajan's replies.

In this honorable world of Pliny's it is clear that the emperor belongs. There is an excellent understanding between them. Any little favor Pliny asks is sure to be granted. When his wife has to make a hurried journey, he allows her to use the imperial post-horses and writes to Trajan, explaining that there was not sufficient time to ask permission. Trajan answers: "You did me justice, my dearest Pliny, in confiding in my affection toward you." Yet for all this kindness on the emperor's part, the two are not intimate friends. Pliny is a literary man whose interests are studious. He writes to the emperor with a flourish: "May this and many succeeding birthdays be attended, Sir, with the highest felicity to you; and may you, in the midst of an uninterrupted course of health and prosperity, be still adding to the increase of that immortal glory which your virtues justly merit." Trajan answers: "Your wishes, my dearest Pliny, for my enjoyment of many happy birthdays amidst the glory and prosperity of the republic were extremely agreeable to me." It is simple. It is dignified. It covers the subject. When it has done so, however, the letter is finished. Trajan, a man of action, wastes no words.

This kind of response on Trajan's part is everywhere characteristic. It is quite remarkable to see what a number of subjects Pliny consults the Emperor about. In every case Trajan sends a brief, decisive answer, frequently after study of precedent or consultation with some expert. Hardly ever does he suggest that Pliny had been sent out to decide things for himself. Anything which remotely concerns the Emperor's prestige must be referred to him. Pliny, for instance, writes to him about the Christians. These subversive traitors have increased in Bithynia to such an extent that in some parts the temples are quite deserted. What is Pliny to do? He has not been present at any trials of Christians and does not know much about the sect. Some whom he has examined admit they were Christians once, but say that they now are not so. Others, owning themselves Christians, have consented to sacrifice to the Emperor after being threatened with punishment. Should he punish these for their past crime? What should he do about anonymous accusations? Should he take pains to ferret out members of the sect or let them alone until they are brought to his attention?

To all these queries, the Emperor, allowing for his point of view, gives a wise and tolerant answer. Past crimes may be ignored, as long as at present the accused is loyal. Pliny should not go out of his way to look for Christians, and anonymous accusations are to be disregarded. But if a man properly accused does own himself a Christian and does persist in this, he must be punished.

In these exchanges with Pliny, the Emperor's character stands out. He is decisive, sensible, industrious, clearly intimate with a different set than Pliny's, yet well able to appreciate that conscientious man. He is in addition very much the absolute monarch. It is not that he ever puts on airs, but that seemingly trivial details must be brought to his personal attention. The army is his, so that when two runaway slaves are discovered in the local forces, he has to be asked what should be done with them. A man has buried his wife and son in a monument in which he has placed the Emperor's image. Is this lèse-majesté? One may imagine that the health of an emperor must be good and his secretarial staff efficient if such matters were constantly referred to him from throughout the empire.

Such qualities in Trajan have justly given him the name of a great administrator. It is not, however, chiefly on these that his fame rests. He was primarily a military man. Before arriving in Rome at all, he had spent a season on the Danube; and here it was that he was to make his reputation.

The Roman frontiers of Augustus's day had been rounded by his successors in minor ways, among which the conquest of Britain and the straightening of the line between Rhine and Danube may stand out. There had, however, been no massed assault on the barbarians pressing down from the far North or the steppes of Russia. As far as their immediate neighbors across the rivers were concerned, the Romans acted by negotiation and trade to keep them divided. Among the Germans, whose tribal divisions were many, this policy had been successful enough. Across the Danube, however, in the Rumanian plain and among the foothills of the Carpathians lived a more homogeneous tribe, the Dacians, who had been brought into subjection by a very vigorous king in the time of Domitian. Domitian, who was drawn into campaigns on this frontier, was reluctant to embark on a grandiose effort to extend the Roman empire over the river. He had compromised, therefore, by paying King Decebalus an annual subsidy to keep the peace. It was not a successful arrangement and was felt to be humiliating for the Romans. Meanwhile, the development of the whole of Thrace was held up by the dangers of barbarian incursions.

Trajan, who had spent his career on the Roman frontiers, saw the problem differently from Domitian. A campaign could be won, and there was much to be said for tracing the boundary along mountains rather than rivers. Trajan's preliminary arrangements were made in the first year of his accession. Roads needed building behind the present frontier. Troops must be inspected and brought up to strength. Trajan was one of those military men with a memory for faces who knew his soldiers by their nicknames. It was important to him that the spirit of his army should be high. His generals were chosen out of the ranks of professionals like himself with no thought of their origin. One of them, for instance, was a Moor.

The war did not break out for a few years, after which the conquest of Dacia took time. King Decebalus, though no match for the trained legions, was a fighter not to be despised on his own ground. He was, moreover, a king of considerable resources, not merely in manpower, but in wealth. Gold mines in the region were very extensively worked, and there were silver mines as well. Dacian resistance was of the bitterest, so that the pacification of the region took the form at last of wholesale extermination or expulsion. Dacia was added to the Roman Empire and was peopled by a mixed race, introducing the benefits of peaceful trade and Roman civilization. The victorious Trajan acquired an immense plunder in gold, not to mention silver, and the mines whence both were extracted. Fifty thousand prisoners, very warlike men, were for the most part reserved for the gladiatorial shows in the victory celebrations, which lasted for nearly a third of a year. A more permanent memorial was Trajan's column, round which in an upward-circling band, a sculptor has portrayed the history of the whole Dacian campaign. The figures, naturalistically carved, show us the Romans and the Dacians, each in their armor, the bridges built by the army, the engines accompanying them, the generals, and Trajan himself, directing all.

The Dacian wars lasted for eight years, ending in 109. The immediate outcome of the victory was a great increase in building throughout the Empire. Trajan, perhaps for the first time, had money to spend. The difficulties of Nerva, the expenses of his own campaign were now behind him. With the gold of Dacia in his treasury and a regular income from the mines, he could afford public works.

He had always known the importance of roads, particularly in the wilder areas behind the frontier. Italian roads, too, were in need of repair. Rome herself still had no satisfactory harbor. Ostia at the mouth of the Tiber had been built up by Claudius and protected by a mole. Its size, however, was far from adequate. Trajan excavated an inner harbor which he surrounded by warehouse buildings. At the same time, he provided two additional harbors on the northeast and northwestern coasts of the peninsula, where there had so far been none. In Rome itself, besides carrying on works begun by Nerva to control the Tiber floods and improve the water system, Trajan built new baths, an aqueduct, an arena for naval combats, and the huge Forum of Trajan, five times the area of the Forum of Augustus, and containing two libraries, a basilica, and a temple as well as great colonnades and surrounding buildings.

In the provinces much was done also — how much by Trajan and how much by private citizens, it is impossible to say. At all events Trajan encouraged generosity, enacting that once a man had promised anything to his city (seeking possibly to gain popularity and be elected a magistrate), he must provide it. In many cases, public works were of such a nature that they suggested the Emperor personally had ordered their completion. Among such are the overhaul of the Spanish roads, the great bridge over the Danube, others in Spain and Africa, numerous aqueducts, a canal between the Nile and the Red Sea. Everywhere a great revival of energy was felt. Measures were taken to correct the declining Italian birthrate, to reform some burdensome taxes. The Roman Empire hummed with activity, as it had done under Augustus.

The Parthian War, which broke out in 113, was less successful. The Flavian emperors, by dispensing with dependent kings in the East, had extended the borders of Rome to the Upper Euphrates. Trajan painlessly added Arabia, on the borders of the Red Sea, to his dominions. Such measures did not greatly disturb the balance of power in the East, since the places annexed had always been under Roman domination. They did, however, bring Roman administrators into direct contact with the Parthians. With the Parthian Empire, the Romans had been more or less at enmity since before Marcus Crassus went East to gain military power to counterbalance Caesar's and perished, together with his army. It followed, therefore, that the chief reason an uneasy peace persisted was the perennial weakness of the Parthian kings on their throne. If any one of them could exterminate for a time all possible rivals, he was likely to turn his interests westward. The situation was complicated by the fact that Armenia, which bordered on the Roman Cappadocia, was, since the time of Nero, ruled by a king who was chosen by the Parthians, but officially granted his throne by the Romans. It eventually happened that a new Parthian king, not liking the present incumbent of Armenia, replaced him by his own nominee. He thus, it was obvious, offended the Romans.

In such a way the war with Parthia opened. By this time Trajan was sixty years of age and not too well. His ambitions, however, were great; while the fabulous conquests of Alexander still tempted by their glamour. Not content with restoring the situation in Armenia, he advanced boldly into the heart of the Parthian Empire, Mesopotamia.

His success was immediate. The capital of Parthia was taken. The king fled. Trajan penetrated to the shores of the Persian Gulf, so that the trade route between Rome and the Far East fell into his hands.

Mesopotamia was quickly won and as quickly endangered. Behind Trajan, the conquered province rose in revolt, while the king of Parthia appeared from the hinterland with a fresh army. One of Trajan's generals was surprised and destroyed. The situation was not irretrievable, and Trajan recovered his losses. But the Empire, which had been feeling the strain of war, provided fresh troubles.

A revolt of the Jews, starting in Cyrene of Asia Minor, spread rapidly all over the East and in especial to Alexandria, greatest of Jewish and Greek cities. It was a fiercely fanatical war with no quarter given, product of the intense hatred between Jew and Greek which plagued the East. Whole provinces were soon aflame. In Syria, which was Trajan's own base, the trouble was acute. Meanwhile, there were rumblings from far Britain and from the lower Danube. Trajan had taken legions from his more peaceful frontiers for the purposes of the Parthian War. It seemed that he might lose his grip on them.

Trajan held on to his conquests. He took measures to subdue the Jews. He wintered in Antioch and planned another campaign. He was suffering, however, from dropsy; and now he had a stroke. Reluctantly he left the war in charge of his cousin Hadrian and set out for Rome. Before, however, he had made more than a few days' progress, he took a turn for the worse. About a week later, leaving all his eastern plans in the air, Trajan died.

HADRIAN

Publius Aelius Hadrianus, A.D. 76–138

AMONG the relatives of Trajan in Italica was a first cousin, a certain Hadrianus Afer, who was well connected in Rome and himself of senatorial rank. He died, however, at the age of forty, leaving a ten-year-old son to the joint guardianship of Trajan and Attianus, a wealthy man belonging to the Knightly order. Trajan was at the time serving in Spain. He was also childless, and his wife Plotina loved the boy from the first. It was not, however, considered fitting for young Hadrian, as the child was called, to pursue his education in the provinces. His guardians sent him to Rome for five years, where he plunged into the usual studies for a boy of his age with more than the usual enthusiasm. His fellows soon nicknamed him "The Little Greek," and it is said his Greek became actually better than his slightly provincial Latin. At all events, his guardians kept an eye on him and at the age of fifteen returned him to Italica, where he was enrolled in the municipal corps of youths for military training.

Italica was by no means a dull place. Second only to Córdoba in Further Spain, it was a garrison town and at times the residence of the Roman governor. It is reasonable to

see 164

assume that in Hadrian's youth it possessed a stately forum, an amphitheater, baths, and aqueduct, though most of these would be on a smaller scale than its present ruins. All the same, it was a provincial town and must have seemed cramped after Rome. Hadrian, as it happened, was of a restless disposition. Tall, athletic, and vigorous, he did not dislike the military training; but it did not keep him sufficiently busy. He formed a passion for hunting, which was a dangerous sport when the quarry was lion or bear and the weapons were spear or arrow. Romans rode without stirrups, too; and the firm seat of Hadrian became famous. He also distinguished himself by careless extravagance, another way of letting off steam. Such vagaries were not pleasing to his sensible, practical guardian, who summoned him to Rome when he was about seventeen. Hadrian from this time on was a part of Trajan's household, yet the relation between the two was somewhat cool.

There was little seriously wrong with Hadrian's character. It was merely that he did not commend himself to a plain soldier. Hadrian was vivid, distinguished-looking, and handsome. He was also talkative, tactless, and vain. His intellectual appetites were enormous. Instead of confining himself to literature and oratory, as was the fashion of the day, he studied mathematics, medicine, astronomy. His enthusiasm for every form of art was passionate. He sang and played the lyre and was an amateur sculptor, painter, and architect as well. So learned was he in the theory of music that later he could debate on equal terms with the famous professors of Alexandria.

Abilities of this sort might be wasted on Trajan, but they were not so on the ladies of his household. With Plotina, with Marciana, Trajan's sister, and with Matidia, his niece, Hadrian was on terms of the greatest intimacy. Meanwhile, he was starting on the career which would presumably lead him through the consulship to trusted offices in the service of the State. There was a minor magistracy open to very young men who presided over jury courts under the supervision of a praetor and dealt with civil suits about inheritance and similar matters. The work was not arduous and gave time for plenty of study. It was possibly now that Hadrian added to his other interests a detailed knowledge of law and legal procedure. At all events, he played his part well and was granted, either through Trajan's influence or as a compliment to his dead father, other positions, ceremonial in nature, which were usually given to young men whom the Emperor wished to honor.

The following year he left Rome and started, no doubt by Trajan's arrangement, on a military career. He spent two years with different legions on the Danube and once again seems to have got into some trouble. The truth was, deprived of intellectual pursuits, Hadrian took refuge in extravagances, seeking excitement.

Hadrian was still on the mouth of the Danube with the Fifth Legion when Domitian was assassinated and when Nerva proclaimed his adoption of Trajan. Hadrian's own position was at once transformed. The future Emperor was childless, and his ward was the nearest thing to a son that he possessed. Plotina at least felt toward him like a mother. It

was only natural that the Lower Danube legions should se-
lect Hadrian to carry their congratulations to Trajan. It was
natural also that Trajan should not send him back. The
young man was too important now to be wasted on a remote frontier. He belonged under the future Emperor's eye.

Here he nominally still was when Nerva died. It chanced,
however, that Trajan had a general oversight over the whole
Rhine frontier and was at the moment with the Lower German army in Cologne. Hadrian, left behind in Upper Germany, was serving with the Twenty-second Legion under
the command of Servianus. Thus when the news arrived
from Rome that Trajan was now Emperor, he was not there
to receive it. Hadrian, whose pleasure and excitement must
have been great, wished to set out in person and bear his
cousin the news. Servianus, however, was a friend of Trajan's and a man who had his own ambitions. No doubt the
position of this ward and cousin of Trajan's household did
not please him. Unable, or perhaps unwilling to refuse
permission, he allowed the young man to go. He took the
precaution, however, of sawing half through the pole of his
chariot, so that it broke on the journey, leaving him
stranded. Meanwhile, Servianus despatched a messenger of
his own. But Hadrian, long-legged and famous on foot as
well as on horseback, continued his journey undeterred and
won the race.

Servianus, who was a soldier of the old school, revenged
himself by complaining to Trajan of Hadrian's debts and
extravagances. A coolness between the two arose. Sura, how-

ever, the Spaniard who had recommended Trajan to Nerva, took an interest in his young compatriot. It is possible that he saw Hadrian's abilities more clearly than Trajan did. At all events, when Trajan left the frontier to go to Rome, he did take Hadrian with him. A year or two later, he married him to Sabina, his own great-niece and daughter of Matidia. This distinction, however, was made less palatable because Hadrian's own sister about this time was married to Servianus. In addition, later gossip says that there was enmity between Hadrian and Sabina, that he hated her. It does not seem probable. No doubt he was not a passionate lover, and they had no children. He honored her, however, both before and after Trajan's death. On his many journeys he took Sabina with him, though he might well have left her in Rome. When he became Emperor, she shared his title. When she died, he made her a goddess. This marriage of ambition, in fact, may count as a success, though Sabina never had the influence with Hadrian that Plotina did with Trajan.

In any case, Hadrian was still more intimately a member of the Emperor's household. He was soon entrusted with confidential jobs. When his time came to serve as quaestor, for instance, he was attached to Trajan's personal service. Among other duties, he read to the Senate the Emperor's messages. It is said that his provincial accent, encouraged possibly by years of frontier service, provoked cruel laughter. Hadrian took up the study of Latin as he previously had done of Greek, and he acquired considerable polish. Later he was put in charge of the Senate's records and used his position to perfect a detailed knowledge of its procedures. In other words, his career went prosperously; while his restless, inquiring mind gained information.

His relationship to Trajan was cordial, and yet nothing was ever said about adopting him or singling him out as the successor. Truth was, Trajan was under considerable pressure from Servianus and other military men who were jealous of Hadrian. They looked upon themselves as understanding the problems of empire. They were the people brought up in Trajan's own school. Their contention, however, that they alone knew how to manage was seriously damaged when Hadrian turned out to have military gifts. Trajan took him with him to the Dacian wars. He was not, it is true, yet entrusted with large responsibilities. He served, however, as commander of the First Legion and was honored for brilliant personal feats as well as good generalship. Trajan presented him with a special token, a ring which had been Nerva's.

Even now Trajan made no sign about the future. He appointed his cousin to a critical Danube command which was often used in the training of members of the royal house. Hadrian handled his problems well, restrained border raids, kept discipline, controlled his civilian officials, and set limits to the exactions of imperial financial agents. Clearly he was an administrator of the first rank. Yet when the time came for him to serve as consul, he was not appointed one of the consuls of the year, but merely one of the extra consuls which by now it was the custom to put in office for a few months so that they might go on to proconsular appointments. In other words, Hadrian obtained his promotion but without the honor which in general attended those whom the Emperor favored. It looks as though the military party had gained Trajan's ear during Hadrian's absence abroad.

By now it was clear to all that there were two parties in the State. Trajan's reluctance to take the final step of adopting his cousin was encouraging faction. On the one side Plotina, enormously important, favored Hadrian. On the other, Servianus and the leading generals of the day found Hadrian too much of an aesthete and too unreliable. His sharp-tongued wit made enemies of them, and his abilities only increased their suspicions. Nothing but the strong character of Trajan himself prevented a struggle of the bitterest kind between the two sets of claimants.

By about the end of the Dacian wars, Sura died. He had been a good friend to Hadrian and a wise counselor to Trajan. Strangely, however, his disappearance brought the two men closer together. Sura had been accustomed to write Trajan's official speeches, since that plain, blunt man had no oratorical tricks. Now Trajan gave this position to Hadrian himself, no doubt quite simply because he was fittest for it. Notwithstanding, this marks an increase of familiarity and a glimpse for Hadrian into some of the secrets of imperial business.

One more great honor came Hadrian's way. In the year 111, the Athenians asked permission to elect Hadrian to the board of archons which traditionally governed the city. It was their highest compliment and, Athens being the university of the world, an exceptional one. No member of the imperial houses but Domitian had ever been granted it. No doubt Hadrian was far the most suitable candidate for such an office which the Empire had produced. His wide culture, his devotion to all things Greek, even his affecting a beard in the manner of philosophers fitted him for it. Notwithstanding, it was an unusual honor and required the special permission of Trajan. This was granted. Hadrian paid a visit to Athens and made a tour of Greece. The Athenians placed his statue in the theater of Dionysus. Everybody must have seen that Hadrian had been specially marked out. Trajan was growing older, and it was time he named his heir. But still he did not do so.

The outbreak of the Parthian War in 113 was in itself a triumph for the military group. The policy of expansion which had paid such big dividends in Dacia was to be resumed. The spectacular successes of Trajan in the early part of the war seemed to confirm his generals' optimism. Trajan had added Armenia and Mesopotamia to the Empire. He was receiving ambassadors from India. Alexander and the conquest of the fabulous East were on every tongue.

As the generals rose in power, however, so did Hadrian. He was, it was understood, against the war. Naturally, however, his services were Trajan's to command. Hadrian was now in his late thirties with experience behind him. He was fit for great things. Trajan appointed him Governor of Syria, which was his base for the war. Such matters as supply, recruiting, training, winter quarters fell extensively into Hadrian's hands. He became as essential as the generals themselves to the campaign, while his power extended over the whole of the army, and not over one portion.

The war took a turn for the worse. The Jews revolted all over the eastern half of the Empire. Frontier troubles increased in Africa, in Britain and elsewhere. Trajan was ill. Nothing still was settled about the succession; but when Trajan left for Rome, he appointed Hadrian over-all general in his place. Setting out for Rome, Trajan was taken ill and after a few days died. A message was brought to Hadrian that on his deathbed the Emperor had named him as his heir and adopted him as son.

The fact was so convenient to Hadrian that it was widely disbelieved. It was said that Plotina, who had sole control in Trajan's last days, had forged a letter announcing the adoption when the Emperor was actually dead. It may be so. More likely, however, when Trajan was face to face with death he finally brought himself to do what should have been done long ago. His real choice was already made. For what other purpose had he left Hadrian general of his armies? If he had now nominated anyone else, there must have been civil war.

However this may be, for official purposes Trajan died on August 10, A.D. 117. On the preceding day, Hadrian received the fateful letter announcing his adoption. Without delay, his Syrian troops acclaimed him Emperor as soon as Trajan's death was published. It was an unpopular move, a harking back to the time of the civil wars when every major army had put up its own candidate. The right of designating his heir lay with the old Emperor, but the actual appointment was made by the Senate. Hadrian accepted the acclamations of his troops, but he wrote to the Senate apologetically because he had not waited.

All in all, the transition was not quite popular. The rumors about Trajan's last days, the haste of Hadrian, the powerful party of his enemies were all against him. Nor was he ever a man who made hosts of friends. He was too clever, too quick of wit, and far too critical. The Senate put up with what it could not alter, but it had a shock to come. It was announced that Hadrian was giving up the glorious conquests of Trajan.

He had never been wholehearted about the war. He was "The Little Greek," the passionate devotee of that Greco-Roman culture which was the foundation of his world. It was a Mediterranean culture. Why should he weaken it by adding to the Empire ancient eastern civilizations which knew little of it? When Alexander had conquered the East, what he had really accomplished was to transfer to it the capital of his world. Rome, central to the Mediterranean, was on the outskirts here. It was impossible that so loose a cultural link should hold for long.

Some of this Hadrian was acute enough to see. What was more obvious was that the strength of the Empire was insufficient to hold these eastern lands. Legions had been withdrawn from elsewhere for their conquest, and ominous rumblings came from the places so weakened. The revolt of the Jews required far-reaching measures. The very financial resources of Trajan's empire were becoming strained. It was better to use the money for aqueducts and harbors and ever-needed roads. Hadrian was content with the size of the empire he had, and the improvements which he envisaged were practical, peaceful ones.

All these reflections showed great sense, but the relinquishment of glamorous conquests is bound to be unpopular. Hadrian had his way because he was master, but for a moment the age of conspiracies and suspicion returned. Four generals, conspicuous in the military party, were tried and executed for treason. Hadrian, when he appeared at Rome, deplored this business. He had no intention, he said, of reviving those dark days. If the Senators condemned a man to death, they must be free to do so, uninfluenced by anything but justice. All the same, Hadrian's chief enemies were dead; and people noted the fact. On the whole Hadrian was not quite trusted, but he was feared. Rome had found a master.

With his characteristic energy, Hadrian threw himself into the business of managing his empire. Once he had concluded Trajan's wars, it was not too difficult to put down the Jews and to restore order. But there was infinitely more to be done. Hadrian's knowledge by now was vast, his curiosity insatiable, his memory retentive. Restless, probing, organizing, he ranged his world. In the course of his seventeen years of rule, he managed to visit the remotest parts of his empire. Almost never did a year pass without its journey, while for five continuous years he never so much as visited Rome. The imperial roads had reached a peak of perfection, and anywhere along them at any time the imperial cortege might pass. Ahead went its outriders, clearing the way. Behind these followed the sleeping carriages, Hadrian's library, his court, his wife Sabina. In the midst of them rode the Emperor himself, always bareheaded, simply dressed, yet a little of a dandy with his beard neatly trimmed and his hair set in curls on his forehead.

Everywhere there was much to learn and much to do. The peaceful works of Trajan were capable of infinite expansion. Little escaped the Emperor's attention. Even slaves must have their rights ensured. Even Christians must be protected from false accusations. Great tasks were set in hand, such as a codification of Roman law which later served as a basis for the more famous code of Justinian. But the work of the emperor was not entirely peaceful. Legionary discipline was apt to grow slack where a frontier was quiet; and there were occasions when Hadrian spent his time with his troops, demonstrating to them that their tall, bareheaded Emperor could manage a twenty-mile march in full armor as well as they. He knew his soldiers as Trajan himself had done, while with such simple people he seemed to have less difficulty making friends.

While he emphasized discipline, however, he was not wasteful of his soldiers' lives. On the contrary, his fixed resolve not to expand the Empire gave him permanent frontiers. It was worthwhile, therefore, to fortify these with extreme care. The most famous example of this is Hadrian's Wall across the north of England, running over seventy miles from sea to sea. Most of it was about eight feet thick, with a rubble-and-mortar core and faced with stone. In front was a thirty-foot ditch. Its garrison was housed in forts built into the wall, and its function was to patrol it rather than defend it. Clear along it there was a rampart walk with a small fort every mile and two signal towers between each milecastle and the next. Here and there were gates which opened for peaceful traffic. It was never the Roman ambition to discourage frontier trade, but rather to control it. Smugglers and raiders were kept out by the wall, and Roman sentries had a covered way to walk on. Other fortifications and camps of different designs were constructed elsewhere to serve the needs of the Rhine or Danube frontiers.

In these ways Hadrian toured his empire, adding everywhere to its defense, its welfare, its organization or buildings. Like the Empire, he had grown out of Rome. The rise of the provinces during the last hundred years had been increasingly at Italian or Roman expense. Since along with it had gone a rise in absolute rule, the relation between the Emperor and his subjects was becoming less dependent on Rome. This was a tendency which would increase and lead to the splitting of the Empire.

Perhaps in part for this reason, there were always reservations between the Emperor and the Romans. Elsewhere, as was natural in a man who did much good, Hadrian was popular. He was easy of access and his manner was simple. There is a story told of him that one day he went into the public baths and saw an old man rubbing his back against a post. He asked him why, and found that he was too poor to afford a slave to rub him. His was a deserving case, and Hadrian bestowed on him modest riches. The next time

Hadrian came into the baths, he found it full of old men all anxiously rubbing their backs against posts. Hadrian simply laughed and, as he left, advised them to rub one another.

This story is interesting in a number of ways. It gives a picture of Hadrian's sardonic sense of humor as well as the difficulties of an emperor's life. But perhaps the most remarkable thing is the fact that Hadrian, who had a taste for magnificence and built himself some very elaborate villas, should nevertheless attend a public bath where bankrupt old men also had admittance. Perhaps in truth he never did. It is true, however, that he was a good mixer with all classes, even though people found it hard to know him well.

Under such an emperor, the Roman world must flourish. Arts and sciences received encouragement. Music and literature enjoyed his patronage. It was not Hadrian's fault that earlier impulses which had made great art had worked themselves out. No Horace or Vergil was waiting to be discovered. Hadrian's own tastes were antiquarian and pedantic. Queen of the arts in his day was architecture. Roman aqueducts and bridges, amphitheaters, forts, or baths had a direct relation with the life of their day which other arts now lacked. Portraiture still flourished, however; and Hadrian's own handsome face is familiar to us.

The Emperor seemed to grow old early. Perhaps after all his frantic activities took toll of his powerful frame. Childless, and with a wife more respected than loved, loneliness weighed heavily on him. He became obsessed for a while with a beautiful boy named Antinoüs, one of his attendants.

But on a visit to Egypt, Antinoüs was drowned in the Nile, we do not know how. Some say he committed suicide. At all events, Hadrian was inconsolable with grief and made Antinoüs into a god. At this point a strange thing happened in the East. The death of a beautiful boy and the conception of a man-god took hold. Antinoüs was identified in the popular mind with Adonis, Thammuz, and other beautiful young men of legend whose dying and revival by the gods was a symbol of spring. A romantic cult of Antinoüs which seemed for a brief moment almost a rival of Christian beliefs sprang up, and then — because it had no real roots — it withered away. Antinoüs, man-god, symbol of death and resurrection, was only an emperor's favorite after all — a silly plaything.

Hadrian was old and sick at heart. He looked around on the Romans who had never really loved him and were waiting to see what would happen when he died. Dark suspicions clouded a once-generous mind. Indeed, it seems possible that Hadrian was not at this stage completely sane. Men died — few men compared to those destroyed by Domitian — but the age of fear had come again. Among them was his ninety-year-old brother-in-law Servianus and his grandson, Hadrian's own sister's grandson, who might have been a claimant to the throne. For Hadrian had made up his mind on the succession, and he did not intend to choose the descendants of Servianus.

He knew from experience that Trajan had been unwise, and he would not repeat that old mistake. His case,

however, had a difficulty of its own. He had fixed on a boy
in whom he sensed a noble nature, but he was too young.
Hadrian was getting on in his fifties. If he could have
counted on another fifteen years of life, all would have been
well. It was clear, however, that he could not. Counselors
urged him to choose an heir, but he was looking merely for
a custodian, a man to occupy the throne for a few years
while the boy grew. Why his choice for custodian fell on
Lucius Commodus, it is hard to say. The nomination seems
to have caused surprise and disappointment. Nor would
Commodus seem at first sight a logical man, since he had a
son of his own. Hadrian, however, adopted him, giving him
the name of Aelius Caesar and requiring him in turn to
adopt young Annius Verus, who was seven years older than
his own son. It is just possible that Hadrian made this arrangement because Aelius Caesar was not expected to live
long. If so, he miscalculated. The new Caesar died too soon,
leaving his adopted son and his own son still too young to
inherit. Hadrian had to go through all the weary work of
choosing again.

He had better luck on the second attempt. Antoninus,
later called Pius, was a childless man of middle age who was
perfectly ready to adopt both Verus and the son of Aelius
Caesar. He was not a person of great ability like Hadrian,
but his birth was excellent and his nature was noble. Antoninus had to do. Hadrian, sick and weary of life, tried to commit suicide. Restrained, he lingered, melancholy, self-mock-
ing, hated by the Romans. It is strange that when so great a
man died, the Roman Senate was anxious to withhold the

last compliment it was in its power to pay. Good emperors were deified. Bad ones were not so. It was only at the insistence of Antoninus Pius that Hadrian entered into the company of gods.

MARCUS AURELIUS

Marcus Aurelius Antoninus, A.D. 121–180

ANNIUS VERUS, so called after the grandfather who brought
him up, was of distinguished family and Spanish descent.
The emperor Hadrian, who in all his restless journeys never
revisited the city of his birth, yet showed a tendency to dis-
tinguish Romanized Spaniards of the general group to which
Verus belonged. It happened, moreover, that the older Annius Verus was an outstanding man, exceedingly wealthy
and at the same time wise. His son had died early, and this
grandson became his fondest hope. The youth and child-
hood of young Verus were happy. He admired his grandfather and adored his mother, who was an ideal example of
a noble Roman lady.

He early attracted the notice of the Emperor, who admitted him to the Knightly order at six and to an honorary
priesthood at eight. These compliments can hardly be supposed to be a tribute to the boy himself, but rather to his
family, which the Emperor was pleased to honor. It is clear,
however, that he was known to Hadrian more intimately
than most boys of his age. By the time that he was fifteen,

the Emperor's mind was made up. Young Annius Verus was
fit to be his successor.

We know what Hadrian saw in the boy from what he said
about him. His name was "Verus," which means "true."
Hadrian nicknamed him "Verissimus," "the absolutely true."
It was a sound judgment. Verus was one of those exceptional people with a perfectly genuine nature, of one color
through and through. His upbringing had been unusually
quiet and simple. Trained to bear fatigue and discomfort, to
put up with little, Verus was a grave, studious lad who did
not demonstrate any of the superior gifts of Hadrian
himself. His talent lay in his nature, and his interests were
moral. Brilliantly educated by over twenty outstanding
teachers, he later lists a number, telling us in each case what
he learned. It is interesting to see that from the man who
taught him the elements of Greek he learned to refrain from
faultfinding, while from various philosophers, he learned to
tolerate ignorant people, not to invent excuses to get out of
helping others, and not to show off. In other words, character was his real preoccupation.

Perhaps it was not until he was fifteen that the boy himself became aware of what lay ahead. It cannot have been a
cause for rejoicing. His was not a worldly nature, and the
Empire presented itself as responsibility. Never physically
strong and plagued all his life by stomach troubles, the boy
was not lighthearted. He was devoid, apparently of humor.
But though the Empire was a burden to him, it also was a
challenge. Surely his opportunities to do good would be immense. He did not flinch from them.

Hadrian showed his hand during his first years of illness when he adopted Lucius Commodus. He had gone through the form of having recommendations and had received a list of the ten worthiest people. Commodus was not on it. Nobody knew the real reasons for the choice; and the Emperor joked about it, saying he had chosen the man for his good looks. He hastened, however, to betroth young Verus to Commodus's daughter and clearly marked him out to be the next successor, relegating Commodus's own son to the second position.

All these arrangements were upset again when Commodus, now Aelius Caesar, died. Antoninus, who was Hadrian's second choice and luckily without a son, was required to adopt both boys. Accordingly, after the customary changes of name, young Annius Verus became Marcus Aurelius Antoninus, while the son of Aelius Caesar took the name of Lucius Verus. The betrothal of Marcus Aurelius was broken up, and he was contracted to marry the only daughter of Antoninus, Faustina.

Hadrian did not linger long. He was ill and suffering, and his last years dragged endlessly for him. The succession to the Empire was fixed now for two generations. He had even provided an alternative heir, just possibly with an anxious thought to the health of Marcus Aurelius. No doubt he was glad to die, worn out before he was sixty. Antoninus was left to enjoy the fruits of Hadrian's efforts.

Antoninus Pius was one of those rare rulers whose domestic life was a model for his subjects. This is not by any means invariably an advantage. History provides a number of examples of such rulers who, proving unequal to large issues, have dragged their empires down. But Hadrian had chosen more wisely than this. Though Antoninus was not by any means a clever man, he was experienced, and even more conspicuously he was lucky. It is the age of Antoninus which is, not perhaps the golden, but the silver age of Rome. It was the nonentity, comparatively speaking, who saw the ripening of his predecessors' efforts and left troubles for him who should come after. One miscalculation Hadrian evidently made. Since Antoninus was fifty-two when he succeeded and life expectancy was fairly short, it is probable that Hadrian had not imagined that he would keep Marcus Aurelius waiting to succeed to the throne for twenty-three years.

They were happy years in Rome and for the Empire. To be sure, the Emperor was remote from his subjects again. He sat at Rome and must be approached by delegations. He was kindly, however, hardworking, always took the best advice. Though one of the wealthiest men in Rome before his accession, Antoninus was simple in manner, preferred country life, liked hunting, fishing and outdoor things, but was in a mild way a patron of learning. His wife, Faustina, was an aunt of Marcus Aurelius. The Emperor and his two heirs formed a close family.

They were lucky in one another. Antoninus was the least suspicious of men. When two conspirators against him were unmasked, one was executed by the Senate, while the other committed suicide. Antoninus pardoned and helped the son of the first and forbade all inquiry into the doings of the second. It would never occur to such a man that his heir might find his rule a trifle long and be tempted to end it. Similarly these thoughts could find no foothold in the character of Marcus Aurelius. The young Verus was a weaker but amiable young man and after all but third in succession. They lived, therefore, quite literally together. Marcus Aurelius attended his "father" on country visits to enjoy the festival of the vintage on his estates. He admired Antoninus for his genuine qualities, never dwelling on his limitations. Indeed, he actually loved him and took him in many ways as his example.

It was an idyll while it lasted. The affairs of empires are never quite uneventful, and there were wars. Hadrian, however, and Trajan had done their work well. The Roman boundaries were organized and strongly fortified. The legions were disciplined, their commanders excellently trained and shrewdly chosen. It was not necessary for the aging emperor to intervene in person, and he did not send Marcus Aurelius.

Time slipped by. Nothing really constructive can be traced in the work of Antoninus. His legislation was sensible, humanitarian, just. The great impulses toward building and public works which Trajan and Hadrian had inspired still persisted. In the cities of the Empire, private wealth was now providing far more than ever before, though imperial planning languished. It was an age in which men felt not excited, not adventurous, but happy in what they had achieved. Perhaps they imagined that their state would prolong itself forever. But the forces of history are dynamic.

Antoninus died in A.D. 161, leaving the throne to Marcus Aurelius. He, however, insisted that Verus share it with him, so that the Roman world for the first time possessed two people with the title of Augustus at once. If practicable, this was not a bad notion. It was necessary for the Augusti to be up and doing. They were youngish and energetic, and the Empire needed a lead. The task which had worn Hadrian out might possibly be accomplished by two instead of one — if they worked together. Much depended on the character of the younger Augustus, Lucius Verus.

Much that has come down to us about Lucius Verus may be discounted as mere malicious gossip. Scandalmongering about the imperial house had been for a century and a half a favorite occupation. There seems no doubt, however, that he was not equal to the responsibilities he faced. He was tall and handsome with blond locks which he powdered with gold to shimmer in the sun. He was well educated, simple and open in manner. Unlike Antoninus, however, and Marcus Aurelius he had a taste for luxury. It need not be imagined that because the Emperor himself lived modestly, Roman society had been transformed since the wild days of Nero. One glance at ladies' headdresses in the Flavian age may serve to settle that question. Built up elaborately with false hair, they are more reminiscent of the days of powder and patch than of any other save the recent. Lucius Verus, with plenty to encourage him, embarked on extravagant par-

ties. It is recorded that at one of his dinners for twelve each
guest took home with him the following presents: a slave
cupbearer, a slave carver, a service of plate, a collection of
living beasts and birds of the rare kinds served at table, cups
of valuable glass which were renewed at various courses,
goblets of gold and silver, wreaths of flowers forced out of
season and held together by gold bands, gold vases of per-
fume, and a chariot to drive home in drawn by mules with
yokes of silver. In fairness to Verus, it may be said that he
was fond of Marcus Aurelius and anxious to play his part.
He was surrounded, however, by undesirable people who
might easily in later times make bad blood between the Augusti.

To all such tendencies on his brother's part, Marcus Aurelius turned a blind eye. It was his custom to look obstinately on the good side of men, which made him beloved
but was at times a weakness. He was now forty years old,
and his noble character was completely formed. Christian
people are often too apt to imagine that real goodness came
into the world with their religion and is only developed inside it. Marcus Aurelius may give them the lie. His religious
opinions were Stoic. Stoic philosophers believed in gods
only in, as it were, a symbolic way. They really believed in
the Universe, which runs according to its own laws of harmony. With these, the individual can be in or out of tune.
Their nature, translated into human terms, is moral. Thus
the morally perfect man, if he but knows it, is the truly
happy man who is in touch with the real nature of the
world. What happens to him, be it pain, sorrow, poverty,

does not matter. He must learn to be above events, to disregard them. It is perhaps to his credit that Marcus Aurelius
did not always obey this rule. Rising above misfortune or
sickness, he still felt sorrow. Indeed on one occasion when
he burst out crying at the death of one of his teachers, it was
the emperor Antoninus who restrained those attendants who
were reminding him to pull himself together. "Let him
grieve," the kind Emperor said. "Even philosophy does not
destroy the affections."

The Stoic philosophy had provided the answer to the fears
of the Roman aristocracy under Nero or under Domitian.
To the man who is perfect, life or death are the merest acci-
dents. Whether Stoicism also would furnish an Emperor with
what he needed to rule remained to be seen. It is certain
that it introduced a new note into imperial affairs. Verus
writes to his brother about a certain Avidius Cassius, an
ambitious general who might prove dangerous. Marcus Aurelius replies: "If the empire is divinely granted to him, we
shall not be able to slay him, even if we desire . . . Therefore let Cassius do as he likes, especially since he is a good
leader, firm and brave, and useful to the state. As to your
advice to provide by his death for the security of my children, let my children perish if Avidius deserves to be loved
more than they."

The reign opened inauspiciously with a Parthian invasion.
The Parthian Empire, loosely organized but warlike, could
be counted on to make an attack about once in a
generation. Whenever a Parthian king did manage to seat
himself firmly on that much-disputed throne, he was bound

to be tempted to turn the efforts of his turbulent nobles against the Romans rather than himself. The cities of Syria were rich, and plunder was as much a motive as conquest. In the North, Armenia, unsatisfactory buffer state, was a perpetual grievance. On this occasion, probably as a result of the victories of Trajan, there had been peace on the frontier for more than forty years.

The legions of Syria, which now faced the Parthian shock, were also a perennial problem. Unlike the other legions on the frontiers, they were not stationed in a barbaric land, but in a highly civilized one where city living made a real contrast to the spartan conditions under which they themselves were supposed to be kept. Nor did they in periods of peace need to be perpetually on the alert against minor raids. Their very commanders tended for this reason to be second-rate. Discipline always lapsed, and the coming of war found them unready. On this occasion, owing to the length of the peace, their condition was even worse than usual. The Parthian nobles had developed armored cavalry, against which the Romans had not so far devised an answer. The consequence was that the legions gave way. The Parthians swept into Syria, whose cities, left to face the shock alone, showed signs of deserting the Roman cause. The sullen discontent of the Jewish population, which had existed since the time of Hadrian, made many willing to join the Parthians, among whom there were also Jews.

The situation was serious. Avidius Cassius, a hard-bitten general of much experience, was rushed to the spot to take the troops in hand. More distant legions were summoned from other frontiers. These measures, of course, took time; but the end of one campaigning season forced a break. Marcus Aurelius himself drew up a plan of campaign which was to punish the Parthian outrage by a daring invasion of Armenia and Mesopotamia at once. The importance of the occasion clearly demanded the presence of one of the Augusti. Lucius Verus, only thirty years old or so, was eager for glory. Marcus Aurelius was perfectly content to have seen that the planning was good and to remain in the background. Lucius Verus accordingly set out for Syria.

There was at this point no hurry. The additional legions had not yet come in. It was not campaigning season. Avidius Cassius was ambitious and did not welcome an untrained young commander who had possibly been kept too close to Rome by the domestic and affectionate Antoninus. With all due allowance for the awkwardness of his position, Lucius Verus did not rise to the occasion. His progress across the East to take up his command was leisurely. The manner of it at a time of admitted crisis caused a scandal. To be sure, when he at last arrived, the campaign went exceedingly well. The Parthian capital was taken again, and once more the Romans were for a short while masters of Mesopotamia. Verus, however, was thought to show more appetite for honorary titles and victory celebrations than he did for hard work. The blame for this may partly have rested with Avidius, who was anxious to give him nothing to do. But the reputation of Verus suffered greatly.

While this was going on, a fresh disaster struck the Romans unexpectedly. A plague broke out among the victorious legions in Mesopotamia. It decimated the armies in the field and forced their withdrawal. Next it spread to the cities of Syria and to the whole East, while the legions returning to their original frontiers brought it with them. Presently it raged throughout the Empire. All the army camps were especially affected, and Rome itself was terribly visited. It was in fact several years before the pestilence subsided, taking with it that bright heyday of confidence which had illuminated the reign of Antoninus. The shadow of afternoon fell on the Roman Empire. The epic was far from finished yet; but ahead of it, now vaguely seen and dreaded, loomed the long barbarian night. Henceforward Rome was to be on the defensive.

No provision that Marcus Aurelius could make for his people was spared; but his toil was not assisted by his fellow Augustus, who, on returning from the East, gave himself up to having a good time. Marcus Aurelius did not complain. In his view concord between them was all-important, and he hoped for a change in his brother. On the whole, however, it can only have been a relief when Lucius Verus, while actually riding with his fellow Augustus in a carriage, died suddenly of a heart attack or stroke. The experiment of a dual rule had not been a success. Marcus Aurelius was left to bear the burden of empire alone.

Without a pause for respite, troubles had mounted. The barbarian peoples of Germany and eastern Europe had been pressing on the Roman frontiers for many a day. Julius Caesar had thrown them back and conquered Gaul. Augustus had carried the war into Germany and, though he had not conquered, had fought the tribes to a standstill. Trajan had broken up the Dacian power and extended the Roman boundaries beyond the Danube. In these and many lesser wars, the Roman policy had been an aggressive defense. Nearly all the fighting had been outside the existing frontier, while conquests, some small, some large, had pushed the boundaries further. Wherever possible the Romans had allied with tribes on their borders, permeated them by peaceful trade, and used them to fend off others. Wherever they could keep the peace by tormenting local jealousies, they had done so. But the woods and swamps of the North, the steppes of the Northeast were a boiling caldron, perpetually astir. One people raided another, and tribes migrating far beyond the limits of Roman knowledge set up reactions which must needs be felt on the Roman frontiers, just as waves roll in from the ocean to thunder on rocks.

In the time of Marcus Aurelius, the German situation was working up to another crisis. The Goths and the Lombards were moving south from the Baltic lands, driving before them the Vandals and the Marcomanni against the frontier of the Upper Danube. To all these peoples the Roman Empire presented itself as a forbidden place full of fabulous plunder. Ballomar, king of the Marcomanni, seems to have conceived the notion that an alliance between the tribes might permit them to sweep into the Roman lands by a concerted effort. The glittering prize induced his neighbors to lay aside their feuds. Even the more distant Germans on the Rhine perceived their chance.

The war began on the Upper Danube, where the invasion

of the Lombards was gallantly countered by a single legion and its cavalry supports. This was, however, a mere preliminary. Some weeks later, the Marcomanni, Quadi, Vandals, Charii, and Lombards crossed the Danube, overwhelming by sheer numbers the defending army of about twenty thousand men. The invasion came from the Roman view at the worst possible moment. The plague was raging in the legionary camps, while some of the forces which had been taken for the eastern war had not been restored. Those that had come back were worn out by battle and disease. At no moment in the previous two hundred years had the Roman armies been in worse case. And there were no reserves. The imperial policy kept legions on the frontiers, with this drawback that if the line should be pierced, there were no forces which could be brought up quickly. In this case, moreover, the armies of the Rhine, which were the nearest, were soon also fully engaged. The other Germans, perceiving their own chance, attacked. They were held, but no legions were available to reinforce the Upper Danube.

None of these disasters were the fault of Marcus Aurelius himself. He had inherited a system which had never seriously failed since Augustus. Now it had done so, broken by an accumulation of misfortunes. The Upper Danube was the nearest of all frontiers to Italy itself, while the barrier of the Alps flattened out as it came down to the sea on the eastern side, making an open pathway for the invading hordes, which they naturally followed. Inside Italy, they besieged Aquileia, stormed and burned a smaller city, and spread terror through the peaceful valley of the Po.

Marcus Aurelius faced the crisis with firm decision. New armies were needed at once and must be recruited, not from the barbarian frontier-lands, as was increasingly the custom, but in the empire itself. Slaves, gladiators, even brigands were accepted into the new legions. Warlike tribes from as far away as distant Scythia were hired as irregular troops. The treasury, it need hardly be said, was nearly empty. No Roman Emperor had devised a permanent method of keeping the finances of the state fully solvent. The recent Parthian War had consumed reserves. Marcus Aurelius was unwilling to lay fresh taxes on his subjects at a time of plague, accompanied by a series of unusually bad harvests. He therefore sold the priceless treasures of the imperial palaces to raise money. All towns threatened, and even those which remotely might be threatened were fortified. Prominent generals were given wide areas of command. Avidius Cassius, for instance, had the whole of Syria and Asia Minor under his control, since the latter had now to be weakened by withdrawal of legions.

In the spring of 168 when the campaigning season opened, both of the Augusti took the field. This was the last year of the life of Lucius Verus, and Marcus Aurelius did not trust him to be equal to the crisis. Very hard fighting ensued, and by the end of the summer Italy and Illyricum were safe. The further provinces, however, still remained in the hands of the Germans.

It took about three years to throw the Marcomanni and their allies back over the Danube. They were hard-fought years, and crises impended everywhere. Each weakened frontier was attacked in turn. Egypt, southern Spain, Britain, Armenia all had their wars. In 170 a Lower Danube tribe broke right through the Balkans and Macedonia and Greece as far as Athens. Slowly, however, the tide began to turn. Everywhere the barbarians were pushed back; and Marcus Aurelius, undaunted, prepared to follow.

It was clearly the right strategy. Only by aggressive-defensive warfare could the empire be permanently kept safe. Trajan had shown the way, and Dacia had been invaluable in the recent crisis. The Upper Danube frontier had been proved to be too near to Italy. The time had come to draw the line further north, and in the course of this to strike a blow at the tribes from which they would not rapidly recover. Girding himself for a long war, Marcus Aurelius moved against the Marcomanni, Sarmatians, and Quadi.

Marcus Aurelius was not a man trained to war, but his judgment in it seems to have been essentially sound. What failed him among other things was his health. Never strong, and plagued by what may have been ulcers, he kept going by trying to eat at night when he could be quiet and by subsisting during the day on a drink prepared by his physician. Naturally rumors went abroad that he would not live long. Young Commodus, his only surviving son, born in the year of his accession, was still a mere boy. The prestige of the Emperor, affected by all the disasters of his reign, was now at a low ebb. He also had been too long on one frontier, too much absorbed in one war. Finally the inertia of Antoninus was having its effect. Roman governors and generals, long unaccustomed to the imperial presence and

now given unusual powers to meet the crisis, had been growing too great. Thus at the moment when victory seemed
within the grasp of Marcus Aurelius, he was forced to break
away and crush a rebellion.

The rebel, it need hardly be said, was Avidius Cassius. He
had been nearly eight years in the East and had behind him
the prestige of the successful Parthian War. Ever since the
breakthrough on the Danube, Avidius had been ruling Asia
Minor as well as Syria, and even Egypt. A widespread conspiracy was formed in which even Faustina, the empress,
joined; or so at least it was said. Despairing of her husband's
health, it seems, she had decided to throw in her lot with
Avidius and marry him, in hope of preserving the succession
for her son, young Commodus.

Avidius Cassius was proclaimed Emperor in the East. The
throne of Marcus Aurelius tottered, and rumors went
around that he was already dead. Hastily, however, he
pulled himself together, garrisoned Rome in case of a sudden invasion, and broke off his own campaign in the moment of success.

The crisis was acute, but short. About three months after
his proclamation, Avidius Cassius was killed by a soldier he
had injured. Without its head, the rebellion collapsed. It was
necessary, however, for Marcus Aurelius to show himself in
the East, to make a progress through his dominions there
and settle affairs. Fifteen precious months were thus consumed, and the victory which had almost been in his grasp
on the Danube was once again out of his reach.

Grimly Marcus Aurelius turned back to the war. This was

not the sort of good he had thought to do for his subjects
during those years when he had waited for the throne. It
was, however, the duty laid on him. Ailing but determined,
he pressed on with his task. But privately in the meditations
he composed in those years, he set down for us his real view
of war. "A spider when it has caught a fly thinks it has done
a great deed, so does a man who has run down a hare, another when he has taken a boar or a bear, another when he
has captured Sarmatians. If you probe into the reasons for
their acts, are they not all robbers?" So much for the Sarma-
tian War.

His reputation stood higher now, for it was apparent
that the barbarians were being overcome. His progression
through the East had been triumphant, and his clemency
there had made him popular. His young son Commodus had
put on the toga of a man and was ready to be trained for
the succession. Marcus Aurelius, ill and therefore impatient,
raised him to Caesar and by degrees even to Augustus, following the precedent he had set with Lucius Verus. He was
anxious to have the boy with him at the camp to learn how
to handle his responsibilities.

The fall of the Roman Empire may be said to start with
Commodus, degenerate son of a noble father. Marcus Aurelius has therefore often been blamed for handing over the
succession to him. Since the death of Nerva, the argument
runs, each Emperor had been chosen and adopted for his
merits. Marcus Aurelius alone chose his own son, and with
disastrous results. Why could he not have pursued the better
policy?

In actual fact, it is difficult to see what else he could have done. He was, it may be recalled, the only Emperor in all that time who had had a son. Where the others adopted, they did so because they must. And Hadrian at least was Trajan's nearest relative. It had always been understood that the Empire was in a general way hereditary, for which reason the heirs of the preceding Emperors had been adopted, not just nominated as successors. If, then, Marcus Aurelius had passed over Commodus, he would very probably have doomed that young man to death and even more likely have provoked a civil war between Commodus's supporters and those of the man his father had chosen. The last days of Hadrian and of Trajan, too, had been made unhappy by intrigues about the succession. How much more troubled would the end of Marcus Aurelius have been, had he set up a rival to Commodus for the succession!

Commodus was indeed the only choice. It is possible, moreover, that Marcus Aurelius was really blind to his son's character. We have seen his noble refusal to recognize the ambition of Avidius Cassius. His wife Faustina was said to have been quite flagrantly unfaithful. This is very likely untrue. The pair had thirteen children, and during those long German wars, she spent much time with him in camp. One thing, at all events, is certain. He speaks of her among his blessings, thankful "that I have such a wife, so obedient, and so affectionate, and so simple." Suspicion of Faustina is only worth mentioning because, though dubious, it may again point to the noble blindness which he had shown to Avidius or Lucius Verus.

Marcus Aurelius was not stupid, but his understanding of people was colored by his Stoic point of view. The good man is one who lives in harmony with nature. In other words, man is naturally good, not evil. There are many wicked persons in the world, but their ill-doing is, as it were, against the grain. It results from an imperfect understanding of what they are and what reality is. If they really saw the good, they must needs follow it. These were the views of Marcus Aurelius, inherited from a long line of great Greek thinkers from Socrates downward. They serve in part to explain his patience with people. For if understanding is what men lack, they may always gain it. It is possible to expect their natural goodness may assert itself some day. In the case of Commodus, who was still very young, such a transformation indeed might seem quite likely.

Whether all of these things affected Marcus Aurelius in his choice of Commodus, we cannot tell. In the Danube camps of that long, dreary war, he set his thoughts down on what concerned him most, but he said nothing of his son. "To thine own self be true," he repeated to his own soul, saying this over and over in different forms. Let a man do his duty and despise all else. Let him not criticize others, but consider how he himself may be bettered. Such an attitude may be that of a saint, but is it that of an administrator, a chooser of men? One wonders.

Once more, after twelve years of struggle, the final victory which had once eluded him was his to grasp. The work of Augustus, of his successors, and of Trajan would be consummated by him. The Roman frontiers, more defensible and shorter, would now be far from Italian soil. Fresh vigor would flow into the Roman world. The migrating peoples would be held back or destroyed. It was after all a great thing he could do for his people. One more campaign, and that a formality — the merest mopping up — would end the matter.

One more campaign, but the Emperor did not see it. Away on that barbarian frontier, broken by a task for which he was not fit, the most civilized and the noblest Roman of his era died. His son broke off the fighting, renounced his father's plans and all his gains, and started back to Rome to enjoy himself. This he did so thoroughly and in such a scandalous manner that within twelve years he was murdered, dying at the age of thirty-one and leaving the Empire to dissolve, as after the death of Nero, into chaos.

DIOCLETIAN

Caius Aurelius Valerius Diocletianus,
reigned A.D. 284–305
died 313

THE death of Nero had been succeeded by a shattering year
of civil war. That of Commodus was followed by nearly a
century of hopeless anarchy. Army commanders set up for
emperor at will, two, three, or four of them at once. The
final victor perished as frequently as not in a new rebellion.
Hardly ever did an emperor die a natural death. Even when
he did so, his ambitious generals would turn on his heirs.
These civil wars were distracted by the emergencies of the
Roman frontier. It was not to be expected that the barbarians would sit by quietly while the Romans fought things
out. Great disasters had to be hurriedly repaired. Holes were
torn in the frontier. Like the sea through a leaking dike, the
barbarians seeped into the land.

In these convulsions, many things must be destroyed. The
first of them was imperial prestige. It came to the point,
indeed, where the legions actually put the Empire up to auc-
tion and sold it to the highest bidder. After such a transac-
tion, loyalty and authority were meaningless words.

The second thing that died was the Roman Senate. At first
it tried to interpose and was shown brutally that authority

without arms behind it meant nothing any more. It had been a policy, as we have seen, to use as generals not the traditional ex-consuls, but professionals, such as Trajan had been, who came from the provinces. Through the second century, this tendency had persisted. Men of Moorish extraction, Syrians, Gauls had risen from nowhere to be generals in the great campaigns of Trajan or those of Marcus Aurelius. Such soldiers felt scant respect for the Senate, to which they seldom belonged. The balance had been held by the Spanish-born emperors who, though they were provincials, also claimed Italian blood, or were of senatorial family. The would-be successors of Commodus were of plain provincial extraction. Having risen to prominence in the frontier armies, they cared nothing for the Senate. Their reaction when opposed by the city fathers was prompt and brutal. Very shortly the Senate, decimated in numbers, never filled up by fresh and vigorous blood, no longer containing anybody with pretensions to importance, sank to the level of a municipal council.

With the Senate also died Rome, in fact if not in idea. Each emperor, to be sure, preserved the name of Roman. His real interests, however, were increasingly on the frontiers where his armies were. Here he either fought endless barbarian wars or defended his title against other frontier armies and their claimants. He was too busy to remain in Rome, where he was not in any case at home. Besides, the tremendous wealth of the eastern cities was not exhausted yet. The resources which supported the new kind of emperor came primarily from the East, so that his care extended itself in that direction. The balance of power had shifted. Rome, the capital of the world in name, was actually no more than another city, and not even a very strategic one.

Such a swift and terrible decline, the virtual extinction of the Roman Empire as hitherto known, could only have taken place by the working out of forces which had been for a long time present. The age of the Antonines, for all its apparent brilliance, had been developing problems which needed a creative genius with a fresh approach, a mind more original than either Antoninus or Marcus Aurelius himself possessed.

First of these was the barbarization of the army. Long ago, the legions of Caesar had been Italian, though his supporting troops were not. In the civil wars after his death, Brutus and Cassius, and Antony, too, had raised their troops where they could get them. Under Augustus, there had been a reversion to the policy of "Romans in the legions." Italians, however, became more difficult to get as slave labor and vast estates drove out the peasantry on whom recruiting depended. Various expedients had helped, but in particular the gradual extension of citizenship had made it possible to recruit the legions from elsewhere. By the third century, virtually every free man was a citizen, and the soldiers were drawn from the wildest, most barbarous parts, particularly, of course, from near the frontiers. Like their generals, they had nothing in common, not merely with Rome, but even with the wealthy cities whose luxury depended on their valor. Plunder from one place was as profitable as from another, while it was easier to obtain inside the Empire.

Another factor was a loss of vitality in the civilized parts of the Empire. Despite the buildings, the roads, the commerce of the Antonine age, there were many ominous signs for those who could read them. City magistracies were no longer elected by the citizen body, but by the local Senate. Politics had become a matter of indifference to the people at large, who instead were accustomed to look on their prominent citizens as milch cows, existing to provide extensive public buildings, gratuities, and shows. No doubt the liberality of the rich to their native towns was in many ways a healthy thing. What happened, however, was that the towns over-extended themselves. Men beggared themselves to make a display, providing amphitheatres, baths, and other amenities which needed constant and expensive upkeep. Such habits too soon became a tradition. Increasing expenses were demanded as of right from municipal officers, with the result that before too long had passed, it had become difficult to get anybody to undertake office. Meanwhile, for other reasons, trade fell off, and with trade riches. The vicious expansion of slave labor and big estates which had already ruined Italy was now affecting the civilized world everywhere. To these original causes of trouble must of course be added the chaotic conditions which now arose, endangering trade.

The Antonine emperors, and indeed earlier ones, long ago perceived some signs of this decay. The natural remedy, to them, was centralization. When Trajan sent out Pliny to look over the accounts of the cities of Bithynia, he was doing an immediate service and setting a very dangerous precedent. The more such overseeing was necessary, the larger the central army of bureaucrats, the more expensive the government, and the higher the taxes. To the drain of the unproductive legions on society, there was added that of the paid bureaucrats, busily overseeing things that the cities had formerly managed themselves. Nor did third-century anarchy necessarily reduce this tendency. Taxes were more important than ever to a man whose power depended directly on his legions.

As emperor succeeded emperor, disaster followed disaster. Everything seemed to be breaking up. Even civilized life itself appeared in danger. Faithful Christians with only too much reason told one another that the end of the world was at hand. The terrible prophecies of the apocalyptic writers about the evils of the Last Days were being fulfilled.

Though few people saw it, however, there was still vitality left in the civilized world. If things could not possibly be as they had once been, they could at least be different. Fame awaited a man with constructive ideas.

His entrance into history was no more impressive than that of the countless brigands who had so long disputed the mastery of the Empire. The emperor of the period was a man named Carus who was waging another of those perennial wars against the Parthians. He was successful and again took the Parthian capital, but was mysteriously killed, it was given out, by a thunderbolt. Almost certainly he was murdered by somebody in his own army. His son, Numerian,

taking over command, retreated with the army. He perished
on the way home as unexplainably as had his father. Suspicion fell on a general called Aper, who was accused before
an assembly of the officers of the army and forced to admit
to the deed. Before he could elaborate, however, or impli-
cate anybody else, he was himself cut down by Diocles, who
was the leader of the late emperor's bodyguard and may
have been anxious to avenge his master, as he said, or else to
shut Aper's mouth.

This Diocles, then, apparently just another brigand, was
accepted by the army of the East as Emperor. He was a man
of obscure origin, born nobody knows when or where, and
reputed to be the son of a freedman, of possibly even of a
slave. By race he was a Dalmatian, and he seems to have
been called Diocles after his mother's native town. He was
not, as might be supposed, illiterate. His father apparently
had been a trained scribe, and Diocles possessed some smat-
tering of education. Whether he spoke fluent Latin is dubious, though the army had familiarized him with the language. For preference, he spoke Greek.

The first thing to be done was to adopt a fancy Roman
name. Diocles, which was Greek, had seemed adequate for a
general. For an emperor, it must be Romanized into Diocletianus. Other names must be prefixed to fill it out in Roman
fashion. It is interesting to see Aurelius among these. Deliberately this ambitious upstart is recalling the memory of
the last great Roman emperor, now over a hundred years
dead. It is a first indication that Diocletian himself aspired
to greatness.

The next task was to fight for his empire. The emperor Carus had left an older son, by name Carinus, on the Danube in command of an army. Other armies, dubiously loyal to Carinus, had no motive for putting up with an emperor foisted on them by the army of the East. Simultaneously, or nearly so, Diocletian had to beat back barbarians on the Danube and the Rhine, as well as settling the unfinished business of Carus with the Parthians.

The conquest of Carinus was his first concern, and by showing unusual clemency to the defeated side, he won loyalty for the moment. To aid him in his other tasks, he chose a general named Maximian, a coarse soldier with no pretensions to greatness, but efficient and, which was all-important, completely loyal. Diocletian was intelligent enough to reward Maximian so lavishly that he had little motive to set up for emperor on his own. Accordingly, Maximian was nominated Caesar, which was by now the recognized title for the emperor's heir. Somewhat later, following a precedent established by Marcus Aurelius, Diocletian raised his assistant to the rank of Augustus, though reserving for himself the senior position and the right to initiate laws. Through the efforts of these two Augusti, the empire was largely in Diocletian's hands. In Britain, however, Carausius, admiral of the Channel fleet, revolted and, making common cause with the pirates whom it had been his duty to put down, seized on the country and the nearer parts of Gaul. Since he could not for the present be dislodged from these remote countries, Carausius existed for some while in virtual independence.

Diocletian, meanwhile, had been addressing himself to some of the problems which had caused or prolonged the period of anarchy. The fall in the prestige of Rome and the Senate had reflected on the Emperor himself. Since he no longer had these behind him, he had dwindled to the creature, almost the servant of the army. Some new way must be found to assert his position. In pomp, therefore, Diocletian began to resemble an eastern monarch. He wore a diadem, appeared in public dressed in silk and jewels. He required people to kneel before him, raising the hem of his garment to their lips. He separated himself from common mortals, assuming an almost godlike dignity. The expedient had been tried before, by Domitian, for instance. It was never unpopular in the East, where kingship expressed itself naturally in this way. To Roman tradition it was abhorrent. Diocletian, however, had no other link with Rome than his Romanized name. He hardly visited the city in twenty years. His prestige was personal and not Roman. The world accepted this eagerly, for it promised a new stability.

It was clear, however, that Diocletian's position could hardly rest on mere ceremonial. He must give the people security against barbarian inroads, while at the same time he must control ambitious generals. No emperor could be in all places at once, and successful generals too easily became rebels. Diocletian had the practical sense to devise a workable system, not wholly new, but an extension of the haphazard expedients of the past. Fundamental to this was a reorganization of the army and its system of legionary camps. Diocletian made a distinction between the frontier troops, whose business was defense, and reserve armies kept in the rear and constantly ready to rush to the rescue of a threatened section. Along with this extensive rearrangement went a new organization of provinces. The old divisions, frequently large and unwieldy, had always been a source of danger to the Emperor. Large commands were necessary for large wars, yet the power of a general must not be allowed to grow too great. Diocletian solved the problem by taking the direct provincial government out of military hands. The Empire was redivided into much smaller units, over each of which was placed a civilian, a Duke, or a President. Groups of provinces formed a Diocese, over which presided a military representative, a Vicarius, or Vicar, who was responsible in his own turn to a Praetorian Prefect. This latter took his orders from the Augustus. Under Diocletian's arrangements each Augustus had a Prefect. Each administered a section of the Empire. Maximian and his Prefect ruled the West, while Diocletian had the richer and more important East. Maximian set up his court in Milan, which was nearer the frontiers and more strategically placed than Rome. Diocletian picked Nicomedia on the coast of Asia Minor, close to the Hellespont and dominating Black Sea trade, while at the same time convenient for Asia and Europe.

By this arrangement Diocletian established a chain of command. Each man's authority reached only just so far, either up or down, so that a rebellion would need the consent of many responsible people. Meanwhile, by dividing the Empire with Maximian, he had at least made a step toward conquering the problems imposed by its size. If he could not himself be everywhere at once, two Augusti could be simultaneously in the West and East. Maximian, already an Augustus and possessing complete authority in the West, was hardly likely to rebel because he had little more to gain and much to lose. Finally, a conspiracy to murder Diocletian and seize the Empire from him was the less probable because Maximian would still remain.

East and West were still very large, and wars might threaten on several frontiers at once. Diocletian saw the necessity for extending his system and created two Caesars, each an assistant and heir to one of the Augusti. This provided for an orderly succession, increased the difficulty of getting rid of the emperors, and gave to each half of the world a younger general who could be trusted with command because he knew already that some day he would rule. For his own assistant, Diocletian chose Galerius, a youngish general about whose origin we know nothing. Marrying Galerius to his own daughter Valeria, Diocletian at once made use of him to do the fighting for which he had no time or appetite. Accordingly, Galerius served a hard apprenticeship beating back barbarians on the Danube and was finally entrusted with a war against Parthia, whose king was again causing trouble. After some initial setbacks, Galerius was victorious. In 298, a peace most favorable to Rome was signed with Parthia. Galerius, returning to Nicomedia with his victories behind him, found the emperor ailing. Secure in his own prestige, Galerius began to put pressure in various ways on Diocletian.

Meanwhile Constantius, the Caesar appointed to aid Maximian, had been employed by him to recover Britain. Constantius was a Dardanian and at the time of his appointment had a concubine called Helena, who had been an innkeeper's daughter or a barmaid, possibly both. This sort of marriage had become a common one between a person of high rank and one of lower. Constantine, the son of Constantius by Helena, was accounted legitimate. The concubine, however, was not an official wife fit for a Caesar. Constantius put aside Helena, who seems not to have felt injured, and married Theodora, step-daughter of Maximian. His campaign against Carausius in Britain was as hard-fought as those of Galerius. He was equally successful, regaining Britain, and repulsing an invasion of the Alemanni into Gaul. He did not, however, return to Milan and try to gain the ear of Maximian, as his fellow Caesar was doing for Diocletian. He established his headquarters in Britain, where he made a name for justice, mercy, and civilized qualities which had long been lacking among the administrators of the Empire.

Diocletian, meanwhile, had passed on to other problems than purely military ones. His army reforms had been expensive. The deliberate splendor of his court cost money. Diocletian was also a great builder, shrewdly calculating that the glories of his reign needed visible expression. Naturally he turned his thoughts to taxes and thence to the prosperity of his subjects. Here, neither he nor anyone else understood some underlying causes of declining wealth. What the towns needed was not more centralization, but less. Men were losing interest in production because their efforts seemed to get them nowhere. Hard-won riches were extracted from their owners either by a government in which nobody had any voice or else by the proletariat of one's own town. It was better to be poor and enjoy the free shows without the trouble. To be sure, nobody wished to be very poor. But slave competition, dislocation of trade, absentee landlords, and big capitalists were all depressing the peasant and artisan. Crafts and agriculture were both declining. The only people who were really prospering were the bureaucrats. As imperial managers increasingly superseded local ones, the administrators, courtiers, and favorites grew rich.

It was an unhealthy situation, and Diocletian's centralization of government could not change it. What he did usefully do was to make a reassessment of land values on which taxation was based. This, combined with a reform of the coinage and some clearance of pirates and brigands from the routes of trade, did suffice to bring a fresh prosperity to the Empire, at least for a time. Simultaneously, however, a rigidity was introduced into the system. Craftsmen were forbidden to leave their trades. Small farmers were supposed to be helped by the rich proprietors in return for services. This is the beginning of hereditary serfdom, into which the poorer peasants now soon began to sink. Service in the local magistracies or Senates was made compulsory for the well-to-do, thus drafting people whose idea was to spend little and do nothing. Long-term tendencies toward decay were not arrested, though Diocletian's orderly rule concealed them to some extent from sight.

It was with questions such as these that Diocletian was occupied in 298, at which time Galerius wound up the

Parthian War and began to wonder whether he would not rather be Augustus than Caesar. In his way, Diocletian was a ruler of the old Roman type. The actual city of Rome meant nothing to him, but the idea of Rome was still important. He encouraged the use of Latin as an official language, even in the Greek-speaking East. His new arrangements were careful developments of earlier ideas. He preserved old forms while introducing new ones. He avoided direct conflict by careful compromises in the manner of Augustus. Without Galerius at his elbow, therefore, he would probably not have interfered with the Christians.

The spread of the Christian Church had been going on steadily for a century and a half. It was due to more fundamental causes than a common language and the mixing of peoples throughout the Empire. As the old institution of the city-state decayed, local affairs looked petty beside large issues over which private people had no control. His city, or in barbaric terms his tribe, had once been the individual's life. Now he had no exterior group which commanded especial loyalty, and he looked inward. He became conscious of himself and the state of his soul. This tendency had affected Marcus Aurelius no less than Christians. He, however, sought an intellectual answer only possible to those of good education. To most, the solution was emotional. Eastern religions with a message of purification or rebirth had entered the Roman world since the earliest days of the Empire. Christianity was the most elevated of these, the least dependent on mere emotional orgies. During the third century, it had taken its place, if not as the only important Eastern religion, at least as one of two or three which might eventually dispute the control of the civilized world between them.

Christianity by now was not a simple religion which intellectuals could despise. In the Acts it is recorded that the Apostle Philip met an Ethiopian stranger reading Isaiah. Philip told him who the Messiah actually was, namely Jesus, who had proved his divinity by rising from the dead. Not questioning Philip's news, the Ethiopian expressed a desire to be baptized. He was so; and he apparently went back to Ethiopia, since he had been traveling on business. This may have done for Ethiopia, but it would not do for educated Greeks, who asked difficult questions about the nature of the Trinity. Sometimes also, they put forward theories which the leaders of the Church disapproved of, whether or not they entirely understood them. In self-defense the Christian Church had developed and was still developing a complex theology.

For all these reasons, the Church was a formidable, still-growing institution. But it was much more than this. From its very beginning in simple communism, it had looked after its own. Christian aged, Christian sick, Christian poor were cared for by the faithful. Pious people left money by will to Christian bishops for the Church's charities. In the chaotic years of the third century, Christianity had been a protector during a period when the State seemed to have renounced that function. It now employed vast numbers of people in administering its charities, so that its employees as well as its dependents multiplied greatly.

During all this development, the Church had remained outside the State. The simplest municipal office was connected with the worship of official gods, for which reason it was forbidden to Christians to hold any. Christian people took their orders from their bishops rather than from the town authorities. Their relation to the emperor himself had always been complicated by the question of emperor-worship. Diocletian's new policy emphasized in a particular way the godhead of the Emperor. He had placed his family under the protection of Jove, that of Maximian under Hercules. The conception of these gods was in a confusing manner identified with their representatives on earth. With such pretensions the Christians, of course, were out of sympathy.

By the time of Diocletian, Christianity was in practice tolerated, though not in theory. Diocletian himself had Christian servants. His wife and his daughter, Galerius's wife, were not baptized but strongly influenced by Christian doctrines. Nicomedia had a bishop and a magnificent church, or rather cathedral. Christianity, therefore, was present to Diocletian every day. He could only regard it in some sense as a competitor of himself. Associations which interposed loyalties between the individual and his ruler had always been suspect. They now were more so, since Diocletian laid emphasis on the ruler's personal position.

Arguments such as these last must have been used by Galerius in urging his master to move against the Christians. What other motives he had, we do not know. Apparently, however, he felt the importance of bending Diocletian in some respects to his will. By imposing a policy which he wanted, he gained power. Be that as it may, Galerius won his point. Diocletian, who had put up with the Christians in full view of his own palace for many years, was clearly reluctant to tackle so powerful an organization. He could not, however, resist his Caesar. Later events at least suggest that he was afraid of him. Accordingly, in the twentieth year of Diocletian's reign, a persecution was officially opened in Nicomedia by the demolition of the Christian church in sight of the Augustus and the Caesar. The very next day, an edict was published to the empire ordering the destruction of all Christian churches or private houses which were used for Christian worship. The Scriptures were to be publicly burnt. Christians were to be placed outside the law and reduced to slavery if they would not recant their error.

These measures were at once set in hand. Diocletian had insisted that no blood should be shed. At this point, however, a fire broke out in the imperial palace, probably by accident. It was at once attributed to a Christian conspiracy. Very shortly after, the palace caught fire again. Galerius ostentatiously left the city to escape, he said, from Christian malice. Diocletian, furious now, instituted a reign of terror in Nicomedia. A second edict required all Christian priests to be imprisoned.

These orders went down the chain of command to the Dukes and other leaders whose business it was to carry out such things. They caused consternation. Many doubtless were against Christianity as such. But the actual numbers of the arrested priests was a serious problem, and their upkeep was a burden on the treasury. Luckily, Diocletian, setting out for Rome to celebrate there his twentieth year of rule, granted an amnesty to other criminals and made room in the prisons. It was also determined that priests must be made to sacrifice to the Emperor, and could then be set at liberty. Accordingly they were literally forced to go through the motions or even released on the pretense that they had done so. In many cases, authorities were anxious to empty the prisons and make persecution mere form.

Throughout the East, the influence of Galerius was strong against the Christians. Maximian did what was required without especial fervor. Constantius in Britain and northern Gaul confined his efforts as far as he could to the destruction of churches, leaving people alone. The buildings, as he significantly said, could be restored.

The celebrations of Diocletian in Rome were interrupted by his serious illness. He returned to Nicomedia and for a time suffered from a complete breakdown, both mental and physical. On his recovery, in fact, he was so altered that many people did not recognize him. This quite naturally threw further power into the hands of Galerius, who took the initiative by publishing an edict on his own account, demanding that every Christian sacrifice or die.

The list of Christian martyrs was no doubt very much longer than that which has come down to us. The list of apostates must also have been high. But the persecution of Galerius could not destroy the Christian church. It was already far too big a thing. What Galerius did was dislocate the peaceful life of provinces, inflict widespread economic misery, damage the reverence with which Diocletian was everywhere regarded, squander the financial resources of the State and lessen its revenue from taxes. The only positive result was to raise the position and influence of Galerius. Since he probably would have come to power in any case, this seems barren. Diocletian was weary of rule and felt too ill for business. Galerius pressed on him the suggestion that he should retire. Apparently Diocletian was truly tempted by this idea. It would allow him to use his enormous prestige to hand over the Empire without any incident to the two Caesars. It would even permit him to appoint new Caesars for them, which might avert a conflict in the future. Freed, meanwhile, from what had now become an intolerable burden, he might find rest and perhaps better health.

In this way the matter was agreed on between Diocletian and his Caesar. Maximian and Diocletian were to retire. Galerius and Constantius would then become Augusti. Two new Caesars must be appointed. Who should they be?

It does not appear that Diocletian consulted anyone else than Galerius on this matter. Whether he was entirely in his Caesar's power or simply too weak and ill to resist, we do not know. At all events, he appointed Maximin Daia, who was Galerius's nephew, to assist him. For the West, he nominated Galerius's choice, a creature of his own called Severus who could be trusted to hamstring Constantius, now as it chanced the senior Augustus.

The decision was made, and at a splendid ceremony in Nicomedia, Diocletian officially retired. At the same time he raised Constantius and Galerius to Augustus and appointed the Caesars who had been agreed on. He then retired to grow vegetables, he said, in a palace on the Dalmatian coast, leaving the Empire to its new rulers. These saluted the occasion with mixed feelings. Galerius, no doubt, was quite triumphant. Maximian retired in seething fury. He had not wanted to give up power in the first place, while in addition his son Maxentius had been passed over for Caesar. But angry as he may have been, his position was hardly worse than that of Constantius, nominally the senior Augustus, actually penned in remote Britain and hampered by a Caesar who was hand in glove with his rival in the East. Yet even Constantius can hardly have been more dismayed than a certain young man who watched Diocletian renounce the throne. The son of Helena had been brought up at Diocletian's court on the understanding that when his father became Augustus, he should be Caesar. His position had been in a certain sense that of a hostage for Constantius's good behavior. Since, however, the latter was loyal and Constantine himself won good opinions everywhere, he had doubtless looked on the matter of his elevation as settled. He had to face a different prospect now. In Nicomedia and in Galerius's power, he would be lucky to survive.

CONSTANTINE

Flavius Valerius Constantinus, c. A.D. 274–337

AT THE time of Diocletian's abdication, Constantine was already over thirty. It was now twelve years since his father had become Caesar. During that time Constantine had served in Egypt and in Persia, attending either on Diocletian himself or on Galerius. He was an imposing-looking young man, heavily built with thick neck and broad shoulders, commanding, aquiline features and bright eyes. His energy matched his vigorous appearance, and his abilities attracted notice. The assembly of soldiers before whom Diocletian performed the act of abdication had expected, it is said, to hear him named their future ruler. When the names of Maximin Daia and Severus were read out, they were greeted with an incredulous murmur of dismay. If true this cannot have endeared the young man to Galerius, who had nominated the new Caesars.

These promptly proceeded to take up their duties. Maximin Daia was given charge of Egypt and Syria and therefore of the Parthian frontier. Severus took over the old troops of Maximian, keeping watch over the upper Rhine and Danube. His position was nominally that of aide to Con-

stantius. Instead, he served as a check on him. Constantius, now senior Augustus, was left holding his provinces of Britain and Gaul as before. Theoretically, he was sole lawgiver for the Empire, as Diocletian had been. Actually his authority reached no further than Gaul, and he was prudent enough not to attempt more. In any case, Galerius held his son as hostage for his behavior.

To regain that son was Constantius's first aim. He appealed to Galerius, complaining that he was not well and must soon go to Britain to campaign against the Picts. He needed Constantine's assistance.

The demand was reasonable, and Galerius was embarrassed. Diocletian's abdication was still recent, and his prestige stood high. His settlement commanded men's respect. It was not politic for Galerius to put himself in the wrong by denying the request of the senior Augustus. He hesitated, therefore, quite determined to keep the young man but unwilling to say so outright. Eventually, he gave Constantine permission to leave, but added that he should say his farewells the following morning. By then, some pretext could be found for causing delay. Galerius, who was unwell at the time, went to bed early and rose late. When he did so, he was furious to discover that Constantine had used his permission to get out of Nicomedia and was gone, nobody daring to detain him. The young man, riding for his life, was already too far ahead for pursuit. According to legend, he hamstrung all the post-horses left behind him on the road. He was in any case over the border into Severus's territory before he could be overtaken. Severus, unwarned of his coming, unsure as yet of his own command, was probably unwilling to offend his nominal superior Constantius. Out of prudence, or out of ignorance, Severus let Constantine pass.

The young man joined a father whom he probably had not seen for the last twelve years. Constantius was an elderly, rugged, red-faced man with a big hooked nose and a straggling white beard. All his life a soldier, he was chiefly at home in camps, a plain, blunt character. He was, however, just, generous, and sensible. His health, as he had told Galerius, was failing. He had six children by Theodora, the oldest about ten. Only Constantine was fit to become his heir and guardian of the others.

Father and son approved of each other as they had intended to do. They crossed to Britain and had a few months together before Constantius died. These were sufficient to introduce the young man to the troops and to his half brothers and sisters, and to find him all that could have been desired. Constantius, dying in possession of much and hoping for more, made clear proclamation of his heir. He died at York after a last victory, and his troops at once proclaimed Constantine as Augustus.

They had no right to do such a thing. This was in fact a recession to the bad old days of anarchy when every army presumed to nominate its own Augustus. Galerius was angry, but once again his position was awkward. Constantius had been the senior Augustus and surely had a right to name his heir. Constantine of course should have been appointed Caesar. Severus, who was the senior Caesar, ought now to be raised to Augustus. Making the best of things and very probably reflecting that he had not the resources to conquer Britain without denuding his other frontiers, Galerius settled the matter along these lines. Constantine was allowed to be Caesar.

If matters had stood still in this way, it is very probable that Galerius and Severus would eventually have turned their combined forces on Constantine and put an end to him. The situation, however, was suddenly altered by an unexpected reappearance in history of the Roman people.

The Romans had never much liked Diocletian. His residence in the East had been an insult to their glorious memories. Maximian, more blatantly still, though residing in Italy, had set up his court at Milan. These things, however, might have been endured, had Diocletian left their immemorial privileges intact. He had not done so. In fact, he had gone so far as to levy taxes on the Romans as well as on their erstwhile subjects. They had submitted because they were powerless. Diocletian and his successors thereafter had attempted to dissolve the Praetorian Guard.

The Praetorian Guard and the Roman populace had nothing in common except at this moment a sense of grievance. The position of the Praetorian Guard had been a favored one in the army ever since the days of Augustus. Specially paid and specially treated, they had been the army elite. Influential because of their station at Rome, they had pulled down emperors and raised their candidates to the purple. It was the case, however, that in the new army of Diocletian there was no place for them. His mobile forces were his own elite troops. The expense of a military camp at Rome no longer made sense. Strategically unnecessary, the Guard did not provide the emperor with his striking forces. Maximian had reduced the numbers of the troops, but Severus now determined to close the Praetorian camp altogether.

Without a leader, these discontented groups might have done nothing. It happened, however, that Maxentius, Maximian's son, was just as angry as Constantine at being passed over for Caesar. Seizing his chance, he allowed the Praetorian troops to proclaim him and the Senate to confirm his appointment. Soon he asserted authority over southern Italy with Sicily, Spain, and North Africa as well. To bolster his position, he implored his father to come out of retirement and help to save the state.

Maximian was only too eager. He had never had the slightest wish to retire, had been persuaded or bullied into the act by Diocletian. Boiling over with accumulated frustration, he came forward, raising to six the number of active emperors at present competing for the world.

It was clearly up to Severus to deal with this nuisance. Italy was in his territory, and accordingly he advanced from his position beyond the Alps to put down Rome. Unfortunately the troops under his command had been till recently Maximian's and preferred their old commander. They deserted Severus, who presently surrendered on a promise that his life would be spared. Maxentius, however, had no scruples in breaking his father's word; and Severus perished.

Maximian and his son now looked around for allies. It was clearly only a question of time before Galerius appeared to avenge the defeat of Severus. Their obvious friend in these circumstances was Constantine, who had actually been engaged for a long time to Fausta, Maximian's daughter. She had been promised to him when it was expected that Diocletian would nominate him Caesar. Accordingly Maximian now visited Constantine in Gaul, gave him his daughter's hand, and nominated him Augustus in succession to Severus — passing over Maximin Daia. Constantine, no less anxious to win friends, agreed to this arrangement. When, however, Galerius did at last appear beyond the Alps, Constantine prudently held neutral.

Galerius in his turn fared little better than Severus, save that he made his escape. He advanced too rashly and with too small a force, not reckoning on Maximian and his seasoned troops. Retreating rapidly, he found himself powerless and, as a last resort, called in Diocletian.

Diocletian in his castle on the Dalmatian coast had been living placidly through all these events, growing cabbages. He had refused Maximian's appeal to leave his retirement. Now, however, he saw that his system was breaking down. Maxentius had no manner of right to make himself Caesar, while Maximian was upsetting the whole Empire by re-appearing. Diocletian, therefore, consented to assert himself again. He summoned a conference.

Maximian in the meanwhile had fallen out with his son. It is clear that the old man, whatever he had been in his prime, had now nothing to recommend him but terrifying force and savage bad temper. Maxentius had the faults his father lacked. He was lazy, dissolute, and corrupt. The two quarreled. Maximian publicly tried to depose his son. Maxentius pushed him off the platform among the soldiery, who took the young man's part. Hustled and perhaps manhandled, Maximian fled to Constantine.

He was dutifully received, but even his dreadful temper could not induce Constantine to take action. He hardly dared attempt to put down Maxentius, when Galerius with far greater resources had failed to do so. Besides, his own real enemy was Galerius; and he could not afford to make any other. Maximian's position was therefore an unsatisfactory one. He had no authority in Gaul and no army behind him. It was possibly these facts which finally induced him to come to terms with Galerius and Diocletian.

It was now 308, only three years since the abdication. The name of Diocletian still counted for much, and his gifts of diplomacy had always been considerable. How he succeeded in the almost impossible task of inducing Maximian to retire once more will never be known. He did so, however. Since Maximian's quarrel with Maxentius, there was no one to stand up for the latter. He was duly proclaimed a rebel and an outlaw, which for the moment made no difference to him. There remained three emperors to be disposed of. Galerius was clearly of right the senior Augustus and kept that position. The two other claimants, Constantine and Maximin Daia, were disputing for second place. Diocletian gave it to neither. Instead, he nominated as Augustus another general, one Licinius, who had not even been Caesar. Furious at this denial of their rights, both Constantine and Maximin Daia refused to drop back. Presently, therefore, the world was divided in uneasy peace between four Augusti.

Diocletian went back into retirement. Very clearly his system had not worked. What had endured, however, was a sense of stability. Anarchy was now no longer complete. Maxentius's title was seen to be usurped, that of Galerius acknowledged to be superior. If Diocletian had not solved all of the problems involved, he had at least given the Roman world a chance.

Maximian now went back to Constantine, once more an ex-Augustus. The position suited him no better than before. Presently he took advantage of the absence of Constantine on a frontier campaign to seize his headquarters and try to suborn his troops. Returning by forced marches, Constantine saved the situation; but the old man had been caught in open treachery. Not even Fausta, his daughter, seems to have pleaded for his life. He was given his choice of ways to die and committed suicide.

A curious result ensued. It began to be proclaimed by Constantine's party that he was descended from the emperor Claudius Gothicus, one of the more active of the emperors during the period of anarchy. That he really was so seems unlikely. Time and place, however, were convenient, while the obscurity of Constantine's real ancestry made it impossible to disprove the assertion. The pretext was a useful one. Of the four Augusti now uneasily eyeing one another, Constantine alone was not appointed by Diocletian. His father, though nominally in a position to make him Cae-

sar had been unknown to the wealthy and powerful parts of
the Empire. As son-in-law of Maximian and Augustus by his
nomination, Constantine enjoyed a certain right to that position. Unhappily, the circumstances of Maximian's death
made it impossible to rely on this any more. For these reasons, it was convenient to pretend imperial descent. None
of the others had an Augustus for a father, save Maxentius;
while even he could not claim an imperial line which went
further back. Again one notices that something other than
naked power was still important, or Constantine thought it
was. The sense of a regular system had not perished.

The Augusti did not remain four in number for long. Galerius, who had now been ruling for fifteen years, must have
been getting elderly. In any case, he was ill. After Diocletian's abdication, he had temporarily relaxed the persecution of the Christians in deference to the views of Constantius on the subject. He had, however, resumed it again. Since
Constantius's death it had raged terribly through the East,
torture and mutilation being used to induce the Christians
to recant. Now in his sickness Galerius suffered a change of
heart and published an edict of grudging toleration, calling
on Christians to pray for him. It almost seems as though his
superstitious mind had been affected by fear of Christian
curses. His repentance, however, did not save his life. Christians told one another that the Lord had destroyed him.

The death of Galerius left a vacancy which was not filled
by a new Caesar. Various experiments were tried, but they
collapsed. The truth of the matter was that all three of the

Augusti now had claims to be the senior and make appointments. In length of office, Maximin Daia came first. Constantine was first created Augustus. Licinius rested his claim on the verdict of Diocletian. The world, therefore, needed now to be divided afresh, and the dominions of Galerius were bound to fall to the strongest. Obvious claimants were Maximin Daia to the east and Licinius to the west. Since Galerius had held both Asia Minor and Eastern Europe, neither party could well afford to let the other occupy the area unmolested. Though it took several years before fighting broke out, the coming of a civil war was obvious.

Constantine had nothing to gain from Galerius. He was too far off. What he wanted was to drive Maxentius out of his dominions, for which purpose he needed the friendship of Licinius. It would profit him nothing to invade Italy if while he did so, Licinius attacked Gaul. An arrangement was mutually convenient, since Constantine was a threat to Licinius's rear in his struggle with Daia. Accordingly Licinius was promised Constantia, Constantine's half sister, and a close alliance was formed.

This at last set Constantine free to conquer Italy. Maxentius, by now unpopular even in Rome, seemed firmly established as a result of his victories over two Augusti. He commanded a large army which he had the wisdom to keep in good humor and was not without abilities when he would use them. Constantine for his part had kept his army in fighting trim through incessant border wars. He was not, however, able to denude the frontier. Consequently, he made his invasion with a force which was very much smaller than that of his enemy. Well led and swiftly maneuvered, this was formidable enough to beat Maxentius out of the Po Valley and throw him back on Rome. The city, however, had been fortified some fifty years before to protect it against barbarian inroads. It was crammed with provisions, and Constantine lacked force to blockade it, considering its enormous circumference and the size of the army inside. If Maxentius had shut himself up in Rome, he might very possibly have held out until an emergency in Gaul drew Constantine off.

Maxentius, however, lacked nerve. Frantically he consulted soothsayers and was encouraged by an ambiguous prophecy, declaring that "the enemy of the Roman People" would perish in battle. No doubt he felt anxious about the loyalty of his own soldiers if he seemed to be on the defensive. At all events, he made the mistake of offering battle outside Rome at the head of forces which were greatly superior to Constantine's. He was beaten and his army had been badly placed for a retreat to Rome. It had its back to the Tiber and was forced to cross it in hopeless confusion by the Milvian Bridge, which presently collapsed under the weight of the struggling masses. Great numbers were drowned, among them Maxentius, dragged down into the river mud by the weight of his armor.

Constantine's was a remarkable achievement. A task which had baffled two Augusti with much greater resources had been performed by him with extraordinary speed. The Roman world looked on Constantine almost as a miracle worker. Its astonishment was vastly increased to discover that he himself attributed victory to the aid of the God of the Christians.

There are two versions of the conversion of Constantine to Christianity. The first of them appears in Lactantius, who was tutor to Constantine's son and a good authority. He states that in Gaul, before setting out, Constantine saw a great cross in the sky which was also visible to the soldiers he had with him. Underneath it was written the legend, "In this sign, conquer!" Immediately after, this vision was confirmed by a dream. But Bishop Eusebius of Antioch, who was also a contemporary and wrote a very uncritical biography of Constantine, tells a different story which he says the Emperor swore to him was true. Just before the battle of the Milvian Bridge, Constantine dreamed of a common Christian symbol, an X with a Greek R, which looks like a long P, drawn through the middle. A voice bade him have his soldiers put this sign on their shields, and he should conquer. These stories are not reconcilable, and most historians, unwilling to make a choice between them, have decided to believe in both the visions. If it is imagined that these were messages from God, two seem redundant. Historians, however, are skeptical of such things. They point out coolly the superstitions of the age, the extreme importance ascribed to visions and dreams and the consequent frequency of both among Christians and pagans alike. They add, moreover, that Constantine was of an emotional nature, that he was facing the most risky maneuver of his life, and that he had been searching for a god who might become his special pa-

tron. All these things are true and must be considered. It is
obvious also that his contacts with Christianity were not recent.

The Christian church in Nicomedia, where Constantine
spent the chief part of twelve important years, was in the
main square of the city, right opposite the imperial palace.
When Diocletian with Galerius at his side had it demolished,
Constantine was presumably present. He must have known
the reasons adduced at court for the persecution and must
privately have formed his opinions on this policy. He must
in addition have known many Christians. Diocletian's
daughter and his wife, though unbaptized, were known to
be attracted to the faith. Among the servants of the palace,
there were Christians. When, later on, Constantine joined
his father, he was exposed to other opinions. No wishful
thinking has ever been able to make Constantius a Christian.
He remains a fine old pagan, of a less intellectual type than
Marcus Aurelius, but representative of a decent tradition.
Disapproving of the persecution, he did as little as he could
and passed this policy on to his son. Both of them for these
reasons were popular with the Christians and must have
mixed with them in the course of their administrative duties.
In other words, Constantine knew Christians well and was
in a position to be influenced by them, quite apart from
visions.

It is also true that he needed a divine patron. Diocletian
had given sanctity to his person by adopting the name of
Jovius and by bestowing that of Herculius on Maximian.
Without quite suggesting that they were Jove and Hercules,

he was giving the impression that there was a spiritual affinity between them. To pagans, used to confusing identifications, this implied a common nature which cannot be defined in modern terms. It gave Diocletian that superhuman touch which young Octavian had claimed by being "son of divine Julius" and by adopting Augustus, a religious term, as his name. By marrying Fausta, Constantine had bought himself a share in the name Herculius, as being son-in-law and heir to its owner. The treachery and death of Maximian had made it impossible that he should rely on this bit of capital any longer. He had sought instead to associate himself with the "invincible sun," who had pretensions in many pagan faiths to be supreme. There was a feeling of monotheism about the "invincible sun," which made a transition to the God of the Christians less vast than might appear.

From reasoning such as this, it is possible to explain away Constantine's conversion as a piece of policy, not sincere at all. This point of view is supported by the mere fact that it proved wise. When Constantine declared for Christianity, the Christians of the Empire might have been a third of the whole. It is easy now to say that the future was theirs, that the vigor which was fading out of local government was reappearing in Christian affairs. It is easy to say that Constantine had found a divine patron far more powerful than Hercules who would ensure to his successors a throne in the East for the next thousand years. But to suggest Constantine foresaw and weighed these things is not convincing.

There is no good reason to doubt his sincerity, and we

may attribute his conversion to a combination of factors, among which a dream or a vision played a part. We may note also that he had taken another daring risk. He was probably making more enemies than friends and must walk warily even among Christians. The Church hitherto had stood outside the Roman State. Its bishops had ordered the lives of their converts without reference to Caesar. They could not do so now, and it remained to be seen how far they would welcome a different order of things.

While Constantine was settling matters in the West, Licinius was moving eastward against Maximin Daia. He defeated him and possessed himself of eastern Europe, but was not strong enough to pursue him further. A prolonged struggle, however, was avoided by the timely illness and death of Maximin Daia. Among Christians, this was considered another work of the Lord. Maximin Daia had supported Galerius in the persecutions and added refinements of his own. When Galerius had revoked his policy, Maximin had found a way around this by encouraging cities to offer special petitions against the Christian nuisance. This enabled him to move against Christians in the name of public welfare. Now at last, however, with the death of Maximin Daia the great persecution petered out. Even pagans, it appeared, were sick of it. In fact, from the beginning, the pagan world had shown no unified desire to go to extremes. A revulsion against cruelty on such a scale had been growing steadily and now seemed universal.

All this does not suggest that the Christianity of Constantine was popular in East or West. He was taking measures

to put the Christians back in possession of property which
had been confiscated from them. Many pagans who had pit-
ied their sufferings were not disposed to see them once
again become rich and powerful. It was inevitable that a
group should ally itself with Licinius and that his relation
with Constantine should be poisoned by the Christian-pagan
issue. It is fair to say, however, that Licinius hardly needed
this provocation. After the conquest and death of Maximin
Daia, he had lost no time in revealing his ambitions.

Diocletian's daughter, Valeria, who had been Galerius's
wife, had borne a son to him who was at the time of his
father's death a few years old. When Maximin Daia took over
the territory of his uncle, he proposed marriage to Valeria,
intending to bolster his position by an alliance with Diocletian's daughter. She, however, foreseeing no doubt what
would be the fate of her son in these circumstances, refused.
In revenge, he banished both her and her mother, who lived
with her, to the borders of his Syrian domains. By refusing,
moreover, to fix on a village for her habitation, he made it
impossible for any place to dare let her stay there. While she
was thus wandering in want and misery, Diocletian was
sending messengers demanding her. He was only an ex-em-
peror, however, a powerless thing. His appeals were disregarded.

When Daia died, Valeria and her mother thought themselves and the child safe. They came out of Syria and
crossed Asia Minor into Europe, intending to join Diocletian in his retirement. Licinius, however, had no intention
of letting a grandson of Diocletian live to grow up and chal-

lenge his heirs. Nor did he desire to let Diocletian's marriageable daughter bear an heir to anyone else. Disregarding in his turn the pleas of Diocletian, he had both ladies and the infant murdered. By doing so, he proclaimed to all the Empire that he aspired to be sole ruler and would not tolerate the slightest suspicion of a rival.

Diocletian, broken and disillusioned, soon died. Constantine and Licinius fought out their quarrel in eastern Europe. Licinius was defeated but not ended. His resources in the East were now enormous. He had but to retire there and gather them. This was obvious to both sides and neither wanted to undertake the risk of invading the other. Thus the empire was divided. Licinius relinquished nearly all Europe, retaining Asia Minor, Syria, and Egypt. A truce was worked out which, from the continued reluctance of either side, endured for some nine years.

Thus it was that a decade full of events succeeded Diocletian's abdication. It was followed by nearly another decade of peace. Nominally the Empire still was one. Trade went back and forth. After some years, Constantia bore Licinius a son. He had already an illegitimate heir who was a grown man. Constantine, who had like his father married a concubine and put her away to form a greater alliance, had a son called Crispus now growing up and, very much younger, sons born to him by Fausta. Two separate dynasties seemed to be started.

Constantine, meanwhile, had established his position. He had disbanded forever the Praetorian Guard, used the moth-eaten authority of the Roman Senate to proclaim him senior

Augustus, bowed to hard facts by conceding that Licinius, too, might issue laws, and tightened his hold on North Africa and the other dominions which Maxentius had controlled. In the matter of religious policy, he was cautious. Rome was pagan, and the traditional ceremonies of the people had a pagan tinge. Constantine countenanced them, as he must on his appearances in public. Meanwhile, however, he was grappling with the problem of his relation to the church of which he called himself a member.

It was only in name that he was a Christian, for he had not as yet been baptized. This was evidently not from lack of faith. Nor was it from the reasoning sometimes popular that baptism involved remission of sins and therefore would be best applied late in life. The Church denounced this chicanery, and Constantine as far as we know was never influenced by it. His position, however, was not that of an ordinary man. As a baptized Christian, he would come under the authority of his bishop, who might reprove him for his policies or enjoin penance on him which would humble him in public. As absolute monarch, he could not be thus subjected. In fact, his whole relationship to the rulers of the Church had not been worked out. Naturally the horrors of the great persecution had deepened the regard which bishops felt for a Christian ruler, so that they were ready to meet him at least halfway. Notwithstanding, they were used to ruling over the souls of their people and may possibly have been as glad as Constantine was to avoid all problems by putting his baptism off.

However that may be, the position of Constantine in the

Church was an ambiguous one which was made more complex by several factors. The energy which was passing in
these times out of municipal and into religious affairs was
not by any means all of a desirable sort. It may have startled
Constantine himself to discover that under some circumstances Church quarrels bred just as much intrigue, false-
hood, and malice as could be found in an imperial palace.
Though he was a convert, one could not describe him as
learned in the faith. Niceties of doctrine which tore commun-
ities apart were apt to be lost on him. Uncertain, therefore,
what the issues really were, he fell readily a prey to unscrupulous people. When bishops quarreled, it was not clear yet
what part he should play in the matter.

Some of these questions came up in an acute form in the
early years of Constantine's rule. The Donatist Schism really
started as a quarrel between two rival successors to a
bishop. Fundamentally, this became a question of who was
worthier. During the persecutions, various compromises
unacceptable to the Church had been adopted by persons
not cast in a heroic mold. These, now anxious to cover up
their faults, accused their fellows of having committed them.
Thus at the very moment when Constantine proclaimed his
unity with the Church, it seemed to fall apart. To a
Christian, the quarrel was most unedifying. To an emperor,
whose position depended on unity, it was awkward. Purists
complain that Constantine should not have interfered. He
ought to have let the Bishop of Rome decide the matter.
Unfortunately, it was just precisely Constantine's position
toward the Bishop of Rome which was ambiguous. Even as

the bishoprics had fallen heir to the dying muncipal bodies, so had the Papacy already appropriated the mystical authority of Rome, which the emperors had for the time abandoned. Now, however, both Pope and Emperor were in Rome at once. Which of them should have the last word? Neither precisely knew. The Donatists were quick to appeal to the Emperor, quick to realize that he did not perfectly understand the master.

Inquiries were opened, and closed, and reopened again. Mountains of lies were piled up as the dispute dragged on. When it finally ended, the Donatists were outside the Church, yet more powerful and numerous than they ought to have been. Passions had been excited on a large scale and could not be smoothed over. Meanwhile, the Emperor had become a court of last resort. His exemplary patience and goodwill were not a substitute for expert professional knowledge. The relation between the Church and state had made an awkward start.

The final clash with Licinius came in 323. It had taken Constantine nearly seventeen years to conquer the Empire after being proclaimed his father's heir. Now he ruled undisputed at last, part of his success owing to his own generalship and part to the conduct of his fleet which was under the command of his seventeen-year-old son Crispus. Once more the Roman Empire was a true whole, and a new dynasty was indisputably established. It may be time, therefore, to look at his administration.

What Diocletian started, Constantine carried further. He was, it must be remembered, Diocletian's pupil. Court ceremonial became more elaborate than ever. Constantine wore a crown and blazed with jewels. Admission to his presence was by no means easy to gain, and his public appearances were carefully studied. The growing bureaucracy had become more systematized. Constantine, for instance, was the first to create what we should call a cabinet. His council consisted not of notable people, but of the heads of departments. These in turn corresponded closely to those we know today. He had his ministers of finance, of the interior, foreign affairs, and so forth. Since grades of rank were becoming increasingly formal, these were given a title, "Comrade of the Emperor," which later was conveniently shortened to "Count."

The army, meanwhile, was larger than ever. Constantine had been forced to fight civil wars and keep the frontier intact at the same time. He had succeeded, but at a price. The best soldiers were needed for the central force, and it became fatally easy to use barbarian tribes to serve on the frontiers. On at least one occasion, Constantine even settled tribes from across the Danube inside the Empire itself. These were dangerous steps. As the burden of the army grew heavier to bear, taxation became more stringent than ever. The regulations making trades or duties hereditary were strictly enforced to keep people from dropping out of sight of the tax collector. They also had the effect of destroying initiative. Nobody could rise — except the barbarians, who were new settlers and not affected by these regulations. Consequently barbarians did rise and found small competition.

The barbarization, not merely of the army, but of the Empire proceeded steadily.

It is hardly fair to blame Constantine for not curing conditions which were probably hopeless in the first place. It is better, perhaps to see that the old world was dying and a new one being born in its place. The city-state, now helplessly decaying, was giving place to a rural system. Serfdom, the village, military tenure of land were developing slowly. It becomes possible to see the shape of the medieval world in very vague outline. Diocletian and Constantine were in a real sense pioneers, even though it must be admitted that the lot of the common man under them was increasingly hard.

This was not due to lack of concern. The laws of Constantine took account of family life, of widows, orphans, even of slaves. They attempted to reform the standard of public morals by the old, tried method of savagely increasing the penalty for certain offenses. By providing different punishments for lower and upper classes, they emphasized stratifications always existing, but never before so carefully defined.

It was Constantine's desire to favor the Christians. When first converted, he had denounced the persecution, proclaiming freedom of conscience. To this in general he had adhered. As ruler of a two-thirds pagan empire, he would have been foolish to act otherwise. The pagans might worship as they pleased, but Constantine felt free to encourage true Christians.

With this in mind, he exempted priests from taxation, with results which he had not foreseen. Within a few years there was such a rush for the priesthood that he was forced to limit ordination to people of modest means who paid few taxes. He protected priests further by repealing the penalties imposed long ago by Augustus against unmarried males. To the bishops he gave even greater favors. It had long been the custom for bishops to decide disputes between the faithful in what amounted to informal law courts. Constantine not merely elevated these into regular courts but allowed any party to appeal to them from the secular ones, even if his dispute might chance to be with a pagan. No doubt he was dismayed at the corruption of the law courts and anxious to give the purer motives of a bishop a chance to improve them. The effect was to create a double system of ecclesiastical and secular courts which existed side by side throughout the Middle Ages. This arrangement increased the power of the Church tremendously over ordinary men. Along with it went another ordinance at first sight very different. Sunday, it was decreed, should now be a holiday for Christian and pagan alike. The first day of the week had long been sacred as the day of the Sun to several religions. This was the pretext now employed for making it compulsory on pagans. Its effect, however, was to draw the two parts of society closer together. One need only remember how for centuries the Jewish Saturday had kept their people apart from Christians.

By measures such as these, Constantine gradually sought to make the Christian religion a favored one. Yet while doing so, he was drawn into controversy within the Church itself. The Donatist Schism, serious though it had been, now proved unimportant compared to a heresy which split Christianity apart.

No sooner had the Christian religion been exposed to the questions of educated Greeks than it faced the necessity of explaining what it believed. This proved far from easy to do. The doctrine, for instance, of the Trinity may be familiar to us and seem commonplace. In fact, nothing makes it easily explainable in terms of clear logic to people whose habits of mind are not preconditioned. Shades of interpretation arose. In particular, in Constantine's time there was in Alexandria a popular preacher whose name was Arius. Tall, thin, ascetic-looking, earnest in manner, he had a great following among the devout. Presently, however, the Bishop of Alexandria became suspicious that he was not teaching true doctrine.

What Arius was saying was not original with him but was a doctrine which had appeared before in the East. He did not deny that Christ was a god. In fact, he called him the creator of the world. But this creator had himself earlier been made, was in fact the first creation of God the Father Almighty, Lord of all. Now such a proposition makes Christ an inferior god, a separate being whose relation to the superior god was all too familiar to the ordinary pagan mind. In fact, there were now two gods, a great and a lesser. Christianity was not a monotheistic religion after all.

The Bishop of Alexandria called on Arius to desist from what he was saying. Arius refused. The Bishop thereupon excommunicated him. Arius wrote to his influential friends in the Church, of whom he had many, complaining of persecution by his bishop. He also set to work to popularize his doctrines through letters, pamphlets, and even a song. This last, though containing none of the elements which would make a song popular today, caught on. In Alexandria, the workmen were singing it everywhere, and it spread through the East.

It was not long before the dispute came to Constantine's attention. Important people were taking sides, and letters of recrimination were whizzing back and forth. It was shocking to the Church to find itself divided into parts holding different doctrines. Its imperial patron, claiming the favor of the one true God, was no less disturbed. Confusion struck at the roots of his pretensions.

His instinct told him that this was a personal quarrel, as that of the Donatists had been. Unused to speculation, he seems to have felt that it could not of itself divide the Church. His opinion was reinforced by scurrilous accusations contained in petitions he received.

He did not appeal to the Bishop of Rome. In the case of the Donatists, he had done so, only to find that these accused the Pope's council of not representing the Church. About this time, moreover, the Pope was ill. Constantine, therefore, sent Bishop Hosius of Córdoba, who was his special friend, to Alexandria. He hoped that a calming of tempers and some sort of compromise would settle the business. When it failed to do so, he decided to summon the bishops of the Church to a great council.

Constantine's council, which is one of the important meetings of the early Church, assembled at Nicaea in the twentieth year of his reign. Everyone prominent was there save the Bishop of Rome, too ill to attend. Tradition says there were three hundred and twenty-five, though actually we only know of two hundred and twenty-two who took part. Each bishop, however, brought a secretarial staff, including in his deputation the ablest and most learned priests in his district. Many therefore who were not included in the conference necessarily attended the discussion groups which were formed between the meetings.

Two factors gave the council a special importance. It was the first meeting of the Church as a whole since the great persecution. Some of the bishops in consequence were legendary heroes who had lost an eye or a hand or been lamed by terrible tortures. There were men present whom the whole Christian world held in especial honor because of what they had endured for the faith. In the second place, this was the twentieth year of Constantine's reign and called for special celebrations. The Emperor was astute enough to make the meeting of the council an occasion for parade. He gave, for instance, an anniversary dinner to the whole assembly of bishops, presiding in all his silks and jewels, careful also to show by his manner his reverence for the church fathers.

The actual business of the council was not easy. The bishops were able. There were saints among them, but there were also schemers, malicious, or obstinate men. And apparently every one of the two or three hundred was a talker. Free discussion, which had passed out of municipal life, had been taken up with passion inside the Church. Men were drunk with theology. Indeed, it is easy to see that Arianism appealed because of its quibbling logic and ingenious misinterpretations of Scripture. The doctrinal question before the Church was indeed a serious one, but men attacked it with a passion which actually made it more difficult of solution.

Constantine had opened the conference by burning before the whole group the letters sent to him by partisans of either side. He still thought of the matter as one of inflamed personalities which he vainly sought to soothe. Arius himself was not a bishop, but his partisans, headed by Eusebius of Nicomedia, were formidably clever. They were not to be pinned down by references to Scripture, which they could twist to serve their ends with practiced ease. It was therefore suggested by the conference leaders that the council draw up a creed which should define clearly what the Church believed about the nature of God. After fierce discussion, what we now know as the Nicene Creed emerged.

This Creed, intended to make clear that Arian doctrine was not permissible inside the Church, was the work of the Catholic majority. Arian supporters, a small minority in fact, were quite outvoted. But once a statement of doctrine had been drawn up, their position was awkward indeed. Great pressure was put on every bishop to sign the Creed. Not to do so must mean expulsion from the Catholic Church and loss of a see. The Arian bishops were not as a group made for martyrs, and they did not wish to be cast out of the Church. Quite the contrary. Their desire was to convert the Church from within. Accordingly, when it came to the point,

all signed but two, denying their own doctrines. Even Eusebius signed. The two recalcitrants were excommunicated.
Constantine, ill-advisedly as it later turned out, then banished them.

The Council of Nicaea was after its fashion a great success. The Catholic position had been triumphantly vindi-
cated. Prominent Arians had publicly reversed themselves.
Later consequences of what had been done were not yet
foreseen. The Council had provided a high point in the celebrations of Constantine's twentieth year. It was in a good
humor that he dismissed the bishops to their homes and proceeded to Rome, where a succession of festivities in honor
of the year was planned.

Here at once the atmosphere changed. The Roman tradition was an obstinately pagan one, and Constantine had
never been popular there. He had always countenanced the
ancient ceremonies when forced to do so, but his patience
with them was now seen to be wearing thin. Roman glory
was decidedly tarnished these days, and Roman processions
were doubtless more pretentious than impressive. Constantine, fresh from Nicaea, showed his contempt. The rabble
rioted, pelting and defacing his statue. Constantine affected
to make light of the matter, but the atmosphere at Rome
appeared oppressive.

What made him suspect a conspiracy against him we do
not know, but from a few indications we can piece something together. Constantine was an affectionate family man.
He had always protected his stepbrothers and sisters. His
relation to his mother, whom he had made Augusta or Em-

press, was a close one. He had even spared his defeated rival Licinius, his sister Constantia's husband, until Licinius conspired against him again and was put to death. Among his own sons he had made no distinctions. Crispus, who was much the older, had gained a reputation and was spoken of everywhere highly. He was a Caesar. But the sons of Fausta were Caesars, too, though still only children.

Fausta, his empress, did not share these feelings. She was a daughter of the violent, ambitious Maximian and jealous of Crispus, whose reputation stood in the way of her sons. Evidently, playing on the situation in Rome and the rumors which were going about, she somehow managed to convince Constantine that Crispus was involved in a conspiracy against him. The unfortunate young man was put to death. It then seems that Helena, the Emperor's mother, or possibly Crispus's own wife demanded a full investigation. Fausta's guilt was revealed, and her execution followed.

Constantine left Rome, his hatred of its atmosphere tragically deepened by these black memories. The Empress Helena, whose remarkable character is unhappily buried from sight in a mass of legend, left at eighty years of age on a pilgrimage to the Holy Land. Here, with the aid of both dreams and local tradition, she devoted herself to uncovering relics, leaving behind her a number of splendid churches and a memory of wise, benevolent charities. At what moment she became a Christian it is impossible to say, but her achievements in the Holy Land at this time have raised her to sainthood.

This bitter experience in Rome was one of the factors

which induced Constantine to found his capital elsewhere. There were many sound reasons for his decision. Rome was too pagan. The presence of Emperor and Pope in the same city created awkwardness. Rome was no longer strategically placed. The center of gravity had shifted east.

Among eastern cities, Constantine looked at Nicomedia, where Diocletian had held court. He wished, however, to associate some place more specially with himself. Besides, there was a better site available. Byzantium, a Greek city founded a thousand years before, had suffered severely during the wars of the last hundred years, so that its unmatched position had not been developed as fully as might be expected. Possessed of a beautiful site and two splendid harbors, Byzantium lay across the bridge between Asia and Europe, while at the same time controlling the trade between the Mediterranean and the ports of the Black Sea. Constantine's decision to refound Byzantium as Constantinople was strategically right.

The town was six years in building. Constantine had Diocletian's taste for this form of display, and he was determined to make his capital a worthy one. Important people were offered inducements to migrate there, and houses built for them. Once more the artistic treasures of Greece were shamelessly ransacked to adorn the capital of the world. The statue of Constantine himself was set on a great pillar. For the honor of representing the Emperor, a famous statue of Apollo was chosen, supposed a product of Phidias, the greatest sculptor of the ancient world. The head was chopped off this, and the head of Constantine clapped on in its place. A spear and a cross were thrust into its hands, and it was set up, a fearful monument to degeneration in taste. Other pagan statues, meanwhile, were planted everywhere, but as adornments only. This was to be a Christian city. Shrines were allowed, since it was the capital of a partly pagan world, but only as monuments. No worship was to be connected with them. Two churches, meanwhile, expressed its founder's faith; that of Irene, or Peace, and that of St. Sophia, Holy Wisdom. Nothing of Constantine's structures remains, though the church of Irene still keeps its original shape. That of St. Sophia, still on the same site, is entirely rebuilt.

One other structure was conspicuous by absence. Constantinople possessed no amphitheater. Before his conversion, Constantine had once given gladiatorial games. Since then, he had very occasionally graced them with his presence when he could not avoid this. To Christians they had always been abhorrent; and everywhere, except to be sure in Rome, their popularity was on the wane. The current excitement was chariot racing by professional teams, accompanied of course by heavy betting. For this Constantine built a hippodrome of great magnificence and size.

One unhappy result of Constantine's migration was that proximity increased the influence of the Bishop of Nicomedia. Eusebius, a clever, unscrupulous man, had signed the Nicene Creed and kept his see; but he did not intend to let things rest with that. If Constantine could banish the recalcitrant bishops, he could recall them without reference to the Church. What was more, if he banished some bishops, he could banish others. Eusebius set himself to reconcile the Arians and the Emperor. His task was easier because Constantine was anxious that the breech be healed. He did not seem to understand that a vague formula and a cooling-off of grievances would not work. Eusebius, meanwhile, was getting up accusations against the bishops who had taken the lead at Nicaea. He did not hesitate to charge these with murder, treason, and any crime he could make plausible against them. The malice of the party which he led was exposed several times, but Eusebius had gained the ear of Constantina, Constantine's sister. By this means, even after defeat, he always regained his position.

Slowly the cause of the Arians became less hopeless. Their most outspoken enemies were got rid of. Arius, who had also been sent into exile, was recalled, appeared at court, and accepted a formula which seemed to Constantine satisfactory. After a delay of many years, the Church was actually ordered by the Emperor to readmit him.

A terrible crisis impended. Constantine had fairly taken the lead away from the Pope. He had the power to have what he wished done, and it was not possible for the bishops to make common cause against him. The Catholic world resigned itself to what was considered a dreadful defeat. Most luckily for its prestige, on the eve of his readmission, Arius died.

Saved at the eleventh hour, the Catholic Church attributed its victory to God. Supporters of Arius, on the other hand, talked of poison. Constantine, though honestly doing his best in a situation in which there was no precedent to guide him, had made serious mistakes. Without intending to do more than reconcile two parties whose doctrines he had not clearly understood, he had in fact taken it upon himself to pronounce on the rights of the question. Misled by unscrupulous Arian tactics and by his own exemplary patience, he had gradually advanced as arbiter over the Church. The danger of this was seen in the next generation when the Emperor himself became an Arian.

Even if he had seen his own error in the Arian matter, Constantine was given no time to correct it. Already he was ill, and he made a pilgrimage to his mother's birthplace, which he had named after her, to pray for health. Becoming worse instead of better, he prepared himself for the baptism which he had put off so long. He had hoped, he said, to have made a pilgrimage to the Holy Land and been baptized in Jordan. This was clearly not to be. The preparations for his baptism must be — with decency — hurried. In spite of their solemn formalities, they were so. The result was, they were performed by the bishop on the spot. And who should this be but that ubiquitous schemer, Eusebius of Nicomedia; now translated by imperial favor to Constantinople! That Constantine should at his end have accepted baptism from a notorious Arian bishop gave universal offense. It is notable that in spite of all he did for religion and all he tried to do, the Church refers to him as "great," while conferring sainthood on his mother.

How Constantine thought of himself may be seen from the manner of his burial. He had built a Church of the Apostles to be his mausoleum. Here, therefore, he was interred, his sarcophagus lying in the midst of twelve others of stone, each dedicated to an Apostle. If this seems presumptuous on his part, we may remember that he had created the climate in which Christianity was able to take over the Empire. One could not define him as an ordinary Christian, moreover. He was the original of a new concept of kingship, no longer 'god on earth,' but 'god-appointed.' One can only compare such a man to other people outside the regular order of things, whose service to their God has been expressed in new forms.

The verdict of history agrees with that of the Church. Constantine was a great man. He had a creative mind. For the social problems of his day, he could do little. Decaying institutions were not saved by him. Civilization, however, was given a fresh center, a new start. Men had not entirely lost vigor because the patterns of life were changing. Something was possible yet. On the foundations which Constantine had laid, a Byzantine culture, even a Middle Age could be erected.

INDEX